ISBN 978-0-260-49820-5
PIBN 10830961

Historic, Archive Document

Do not assume content reflects current
scientific knowledge, policies, or practices.

DLER & VAN GEFFEN,

HOW TO ORDER SEEDS AND SEND REMITTANCES.

Please sign your name as plain as possible and give your post office, express office and State in each and every letter you send us; this avoids delay. Cash should accompany all orders. Send money at our risk, either by postal money order, express order, cash in registered letter, or by draft or check on bank. On all orders to the amount of $1.00 and over the cost of remittance by the above methods can be taken out in extra seeds. We guarantee safe arrival of all seeds in class condition. U. S. postage stamps will also be accepted same as cash.

SEEDS BY MAIL.

We pay postage on all seeds by the packet, ounce and quarter pounds. all seeds by the pound add 9 cents; by the quart 15 cents, for postage on each package.

SEEDS BY EXPRESS.

It will be cheaper to the purchaser of our seeds by the pounds and gallons to have them sent by express; as the rates made on seeds are 20 per cent. less from the regular rates on merchandise.

ORDERS BY RAILROAD, FREIGHT OR BOAT.

We advise all customers to have *all orders in bulk* shipped either by rail or boat in order to lower rates. If freight has to be prepaid, please advise us when sending in your order
Orders in German, French and Italian solicited and promptly attended to.

Monthly Table for

JANUARY.

Sow Spinach, Mustards, Carrots, Bee Leek, White Flat Dutch Turnip, Purple Top Turnip, Lettuce, Endive, Cabbage, Brocoli, Kohlrabi. Sow Early Cauliflower in a frame, Cress, Chervil; Parsley and Soup Celery, Roquette, Sorrel, Peas, Irish Potatoes and all kinds of herb seeds, sow Cucumbers, Egg Plants, Pepper and Tomatoes in hot beds for transplanting.

FEBRUARY.

Sow Spinach, Mustard, Carrots, Beets, Leeks, Radishes, Turnips, Swiss Chard, Kohlrabi, Lettuce, Cabbage, Parsley, Cress, Soup Celery, Peas, Potatoes, Herb Seeds, plant Asparagus Roots, Beans, Cucumbers, Squash, Melons, Corn. End of this month Sweet Potatoes can be planted for slips.

MARCH.

Sow Beets, Radishes, Lettuce, Spinach, Carrots, Mustard, Swiss Chard, Leeks, Soup Celery, Parsley, Roquette, Cress, Chervil, Large Royal Lettuce, is best for sowing now. Plant Bush and Pole Beans, Endive, Squash, Cucumbers, Melons, Okra, Tomatoes, Egg-plants and Peppers can be sown in the open ground, plant Corn, Irish and Sweet Potatoes.

APRIL.

Sow Bush and Pole Beans, Corn, Cucumbers, Squash, Melons, Okra, Beets, Carrots, Swiss Chard, Radish, Lettuce. Mustard, Endive, Roquette, Cress, Parsley, Pumpkins, Soup Celery, Tomatoes, Egg Plants, Pepper, Kohlrabi, sow Italian Giant Cauliflower, sow German Millet for Hay.

MAY.

Sow Corn, Melons, Squash, Cucumbers, Egg-Plants, Tomatoes, Peppers, Okra, Bush and Pole Beans, Pumpkins, Radishes, Endive, Lettuce, Celery for bleaching can be sown now, but requires plenty of water if the weather is dry. Plant Cow Peas and set out Sweet Potato Slips.

JUNE.

Sow Water and Musk Melons, Cucumbers, Squash, Okra, Pumpkins, Bush and Pole Beans, Yellow and White Radishes, Lettuce, Celery, Large Algiers Cauliflower, Tomatoes, Egg-Plants and Sweet Pepper,

for a fall crop, French Ma
Adams Corn, if planted now will successful late crop for market.

JULY.

Plant Pole and Bush Beans, sow Tomatoes, Corn, Cucumbers, Algiers Cauliflower, Endive, Lettuce, Radishes, Turnips, Ruta Bagas, Cabbage of all kinds, Kohlrabi, Parsley, Mustard, Beets and Celery.

AUGUST.

Plant Bush and Pole Beans, Peas, Cabbage, Brocoli, Brussels Sprouts, Kale, Algiers Cauliflower, Parsley, Lettuce, Chervil, Roquette, Radishes, Mustard, Cress, Beets, Carrots, Celery, set out Shallots and Onion Sets, also Creole or Louisiana Seed Potatoes.

SEPTEMBER.

Plant Extra Early Washington Peas, sow Radishes, Carrots, Beets, Parsley, Mustard, Celery, Corn Salad, Kohlrabi, Leeks, Lettuce, Endive, Turnips, Chervil, Brocoli, Cauliflower, Spinach, Parsley, sow Creole and Bermuda Onion seeds, set out Shallots, and sow Turnip Rooted Celery and Salsify.

OCTOBER.

Sow Onion Seeds of all kinds, Cabbage, Cauliflower, Brocoli, Kale, Leeks, Spinach, Mustard, Swiss Chard, Carrots. Beets, Corn-Salad, Kohlrabi, Chervil, Radishes, Lettuce, Endive, Parsnip, Salsify, Roquette, Peas. Set out Shallots and Artichokes and Strawberry Plants.

NOVEMBER.

Sow Spinach, Corn-Salad, Radish, Lettuce, Mustard, Roquette, Parsley, Chervil, Carrots, Salsify, Parsnip, Soup Celery, Cress, Endive, Cabbage, Black-Eyed and Blue Beauty Peas, Broad Windsor Beans, Leeks, Endive, Turnips, set out Shallots and Artichokes and Strawberry Plants.

DECEMBER.

Plant Peas for a general crop, sow Spinach, Roquette, Radishes, Carrots, Lettuce, Endive, Cabbage, Beets, Turnips, Mustard, Leeks. Sow Algiers Cauliflower in a frame for a late Spring crop, sow Tomatoes, Egg-Plants and Sweet Pepper Seeds in hot-beds for early Plants.

INTRODUCTION.

 PRESENTING to the public our Catalogue and Garden Manual for the Southern States, for 1904, we desire to state that neither time nor money has been spared in a sincere effort to make it of inestimable value to our patrons, not only as a practical guide in the selection, but also in the sowing of all kinds and varieties of seed. The information herein contained is reliable, concise and accurate, the result of knowledge acquired by constant experiment and keen observation.

The unprecedented demand among farmers and truck-growers throughout the South for copies of our Catalogue of last year has encouraged us in our endeavor to make this issue excel anything of its kind in print.

The Manager of our Seed Department has had the exceptional advantage of twenty-four years' experience in the seed business, which at once constitutes him an authority on the subject. Besides we have the accumulated experience of truck-farmers who furnish us with tabulated reports as to the condition, value and yield of new varieties of seed with which we are continually experimenting. In this way, we have unexcelled opportunities in selecting our stock which consists of the best and most reliable seed obtainable. So much so that our seed has always given entire satisfaction; establishing the fact that they are as represented, **"fresh, reliable and true to name."**

Mr. Jos. A. Schindler, in order that he might gather new ideas, spent several months last year among the great truck-farmers in the East and West. The valuable information thus acquired, is embodied in the present Catalogue, which makes it of unsurpassed value to our numerous patrons.

From a local market-gardeners' trade, our business has yearly expanded until we are now supplying seed to purchasers in all of our Southern States. Much of our success is attributable to our friends and customers for which we are exceedingly grateful, and trust to repay them by a strict attention to business.

The raising of vegetables for Northern and Western Markets is now a well established and lucrative industry, and increasing yearly. Our genial climate and rich soil yielding generous returns. Our interests are closely identified with those of the "tillers of the soil," and we will always try to assist them to the extent of our ability.

Thanking our patrons for past favors, we solicit their orders in the future. We assure them in advance of promptness, and a careful attention to their wants.   Respectfully,

JOS. A. SCHINDLER & CO.

THE HOT BED.

Owing to the winters in the South, hot beds are not so much used as in the North, except to raise such tender plants as Eggplants, Tomatoes and Peppers. There is little forcing of vegetables done here, except as regards Cucumbers and Lettuce ; and, if we do not have any hard frosts, the latter does better in the open ground than under glass. To make a hot bed is a very simply thing. Any one who has the use of tools can make the wooden frame ; the sashes may be obtained from any sash factory. We consider a wooden frame five to six feet wide and ten feet six inches long a very good size. It should be at least six inches higher at the back than in the front, and covered by three sashes 3½x5 feet. The manure ought not be over a month old ; it should be thrown together in a heap, and when commencing to heat, be worked over with a fork, and the long and short manure evenly mixed. In this state the ground is generally low, and to retain the heat of the manure for a long time it is best to put the manure on top of the ground—that is, make a bank two feet longer and two feet wider than the frame. Keep the edges straight and the corners firm ; when thrown up about eighteen inches trample the manure down to six or eight inches, then put on another layer of eighteen inches and trample down again ; place thereon the frame and sash, and fill in six inches of good earth. After about five days stir the ground to kill the weeds which may have come up, then sow the seeds.

TABLE SHOWING THE QUANTITY OF SEED USUALLY SOWN UPON AN ACRE.

	Quantity per acre.		Quantity per acre.
Artichoke, 1 oz. to 500 plants	½ lb.	Garlic, bulbs, 1 lb. to 10 ft. of drill	
Asparagus, 1 oz. to 200 plants	5 lbs.	Hemp	½ bu.
Barley	2½ bu.	Kale, 1 oz. to 3000 plants	4 oz.
Beans, dwarf, 1 quart to 150 feet of drill	1½ "	Kohl-Rabi, 1 oz. to 200 feet of drill	1½ lbs.
Beans, pole, 1 quart to 200 hills	½ "	Leek, 1 oz. to 200 feet of drill	4 "
Beet, garden, 1 oz. to 100 feet of drill	10 lbs.	Lettuce, 1 oz. to 250 feet of drill	3 "
Beet, Mangel, 1 oz. to 150 feet of drill	6 "	Melon, Musk, 1 oz. to 100 hills	1¾ "
Broccoli, 1 oz. to 3000 plants	5 oz.	Melon, Water, 1 oz. to 25 hills	1½ "
Broom Corn	10 lbs.	Nasturtium, 1 oz. to 50 feet of drill	10 "
Brussels Sprouts, 1 oz. to 3000 plants	5 oz.	Oats	2½ bu.
Buckwheat	½ bu.	Okra, 1 oz. to 50 feet of drill	10 lbs.
*Cabbage, 1 oz. to 3000 plants	5 oz.	Onion seed, 1 oz. to 200 feet of drill	4 "
Carrot, 1 oz. to 250 feet of drill	2½ lbs.	" for Sets	30 "
*Cauliflower, 1 oz. to 3000 plants	5 oz.	Onion Sets, 1 quart to 20 feet of drill	8 bus.
*Celery, 1 oz. to 10,000 plants	4 "	Parsnip, 1 oz. to 250 feet of drill	5 lbs.
Clover, Alsike and White Dutch	6 lbs.	Parsley, 1 oz. to 250 feet of drill	8 "
" Lucerne, Large Red and Crimson Trefoil	8 "	Peas, garden, 1 quart to 150 feet of drill	1½ bu.
" Medium	10 "	Peas, field	2½ "
*Collards, 1 oz. to 2500 plants	6 oz.	Pepper, 1 oz. to 1500 plants	4 oz.
Corn, sweet, 1 quart to 50 hills	8 qts.	Potatoes	10 bu.
Cress, 1 oz. to 150 feet of drill	8 lbs.	Pumpkins, 1 quart to 300 hills	4 qts.
Cucumber, 1 oz. to 80 hills	1¼ "	Radish, 1 oz. to 150 feet of drill	8 lbs.
Egg Plant, 1 oz. to 2000 plants	3 oz.	Rye	1½ bu.
Endive, 1 oz. to 300 feet of drill	3 lbs.	Salsify, 1 oz. to 60 feet of drill	8 lbs.
Flax, broadcast	½ bu.	Spinach, 1 oz. to 150 feet of drill	10 "
Gourd, 1 oz. to 25 hills	2½ lbs.	Summer Savory, 1 oz to 4 0 feet of drill	2 "
Grass, Blue Kentucky	2 bu.	Squash, summer, 1 oz. to 40 hills	2 "
" Blue English	1 "	" winter, 1 oz to 10 hills	3 "
" Hungarian and Millet	½ "	Tomato, 1 oz. to 3000 plants	3 ozs.
" Orchard, Perennial Rye, Red Top, Fowl Meadow and Wood Meadow	2 "	Tobacco, 1 oz to 5000 plants	3 "
		Turnip, 1 oz to 250 feet	1½ lbs.
		Vetches	2 bu.

* The above calculations are made for sowing in the spring ; during the summer it requires double the quantity to give same amount of plants.

U. S. STANDARD WEIGHT OF SEED.

Alfalfa Clover	per bushel 60 lbs.		Grass Seed, Johnson	per bushel 25 lb.
Alsike Clover	" 60 "		" Meadow Oat	" 14 "
Barley	" 48 "		" Rescue	" 14 "
Beans	" 60 "		Hemp Seed	" 44 "
Broom Corn	" 46 "		Irish Potatoes, heaped measure	" 60 "
Buckwheat	" 48 "		Millet, German and Italian	" 50 "
Canary Seed	" 60 "		Mustard	" 58 "
Castor Beans	" 46 "		Oats	" 32 "
Clover Seed, Red	" 60 "		Osage Orange	" 33 "
" White	" 60 "		Onions	" 54 "
" Crimson	" 60 "		Onion Sets	" 32 "
" Japan	" 25 "		Peas, Cow	" 60 "
" Burr. measured	" 8 "		" English, smooth seed	" 60 "
Corn, shelled, Adams	" 50 "		" wrinkled	" 56 "
" Sugar	" 46 "		Rape Seed	" 50 "
" Field	" 56 "		Rye	" 56 "
Corn on ear	" 70 "		Radish Seed	" 50 "
Flax Seed	" 56 "		Sweet Potatoes	" 56 "
Grass Seed, English Rye	" 20 "		Sorghum	" 50 "
" Italian Rye	" 20 "		Sun Flower, Russian	" 24 "
" Meadow Fescue	" 15 "		Teosinte	" 50 "
" Orchard	" 14 "		Turnip	" 58 "
" Kentucky Blue	" 14 "		Vetch	" 60 "
" Timothy	" 45 "		Wheat	" 60 "
" Hungarian	" 48 "			

If you want to make a success in gardening, use Schindler's Seeds.

ARTICHOKE.

Large Green Globe Artichoke.

Large Green Globe.—The only and best variety grown for the home market, as well as for shipping. The most successful plan in growing this vegetable is to set out the suckers or plants taken from the old stock in the fall and early winter and plant them about 4 feet apart each way. They can also be grown from seed; which should be sown during October and November, and in early spring. Of late this crop has been a profitable one to the truck-farmer for the market, as there is a large demand for them.

Jerusalem, or Ground Artichoke.

This kind is only grown from the tubers and invaluable for feeding hogs on account of their fattening properties. They are the best hog-food known; a preventitive of cholera and other hog diseases. They are well adapted to any soil where corn and potatoes can be grown. One acre planted

in Jerusalem Artichoke roots will keep about 25 or 30 hogs in fine condition; if turned into the field from October to April and letting them root for the tubers. Three bushels of tubers are sufficient to plant one acre; cut to two eyes, same as potatoes. Plant from January to April, in furrows about three to four feet apart, dropping the tubers about eighteen inches apart and cover with a plow. When they are well up, plow them as you would corn. They are also fine for culinary purposes and therefore have a large demand on our market. They are used in making salad and cooked with meats; which is considered a relish by the French and Creole population in our State.

ASPARAGUS.

Columbia Mam. White Asparagus.

Culture.

Sow one ounce for sixty feet of drill. Sow in March or April, in rows one foot apart. When

If you want to make a success in gardening, buy Schindler's Seeds.

two years old transplant into permanent beds, which should be well and deeply manured, and trenched to a depth of two feet. Set the plants (in rows) from three to four feet apart, and two feet in the rows, spreading out the roots, and covering from six to eight inches. On the approach of winter, cover with manure or compost; fork the beds early in the spring, and apply a dressing of salt. Cut for use the second year after planting in permanent bed.

ASPARAGUS SEED.

Columbia Mammoth White—A new and entirely distinct variety, that produces shoots that are white, and remain white as long as fit for use. In addition to this advantage it is more robust and vigorous in habit, and throws up larger shoots and fully as many of them as Conover's Colossal and requires no earthing up, as in the green sorts, in order to furnish the white shoots so much sought after. This grand result in producing a white asparagus did not come by chance, but was the outcome of years of patient work and careful selection by the originator.

Conover's Colossal. — The standard variety: of large size, tender and of excellent quality.

ASPARAGUS ROOTS.

Columbia Mammoth White—2-year old roots.

Conover's Colossal—2-year-old roots.

Prices on any variety of 2-year-old roots: per 100, 75c; per 1,000, $5.00.

BUSH BEANS.
GREEN POD VARIETIES.
Culture.

Place in rows eighteen inches apart; drop a bean every two or three inches. Plant from end of February, and for succession, every two or three weeks to May. Bush Beans planted in this latitude during June and July, will not produce much. August and September are good months in which to plant again; they will produce abundantly till killed by the frost. Do not cover the seeds more than two inches.

French Market Green Pod Bush Beans—Although of recent introduction, it has proven all that was claimed for it and has become to be the most popular variety with our Market Gardeners in this vicinity. It is one of the finest round pod bush beans ever introduced. It is as early as the Ex. Ey. Refugee; but far superior to it; as it produces beautiful long, green, round and straight pods. Does not wilt as quickly as other varieties and is therefore well adapted for shipping and market. We predict that when this bean is better known, it will become the leading sort for the market and the gardener's favorite.

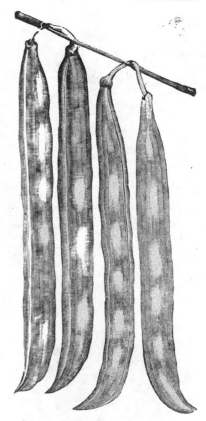

Best of All Bean.

Best of All—The hardy, vigorous vine produces an abundance of very straight handsome round pods which, when fit for use as snaps, are very brittle and of a peculiar, deep green color. As the pods mature they become lighter in color and splashed with bright red.

Early Mohawk—This sort is so much hardier than the others that it can be planted earlier, and often will furnish beans fit for use before any other kind. Vines large, stout, with large, coarse leaves; blossoms large, purple; pods long, straight, coarse, with long, tapering points; beans long, kidney shaped, variegated with drab, purple and brown.

Our Seeds are Fresh, Reliable and True to Name.

Early Yellow Six Weeks—Vines large, vigorous, branching, productive, with large leaves and lilac blossoms; pods long, straight, narrow, handsome, and when young, of good quality; beans long, kidney-shaped, yellowish-drab, with darker marks about the eye.

Stringless Green Pod Beans

Stringless Green Pod—This new bean produces a vine similar to Red Valentine, but develops pods to edible condition two to three days earlier than Valentine, that is to say in thirty to thirty-one days from germination, which extraordinary maturity for table at once advances the Stringless Green Pod to the first rank among table beans. The pods are green, not quite so round as Valentine and less curved. The pods are stringless—absolutely so—this quality at once placing the variety at the top of the list among table beans. While the early maturity is of great merit, this stringless quality is of particular value, the pods breaking as short and free as pipe stems.

Extra Early Round Pod Red Valentine—For snaps there is nothing superior to this variety among the older green-podded sorts, and many prefer it to the wax varieties. Vine erect, with coarse, dark green leaves, and large, white blossoms; pods medium length, curved, cylindrical, with crease in back, very fleshy, crisp and tender; beans medium sized, long, irregular, pink, marbled with red. We know of no stock of Red Valentine which can be compared with that we offer in tenderness and high quality of pod. It is as early as the earliest.

Extra Early Refugee Beans.

Extra Early Refugee—This is a great improvement on the old and well known Refugee, as it is a long way earlier, being fit to pick nearly as early as six weeks. It is more dwarf and compact in growth, while the pods are round, solid, tender, and of the most excellent quality. Very good shipper and splendid for our market.

BUSH BEANS.
WAX PODDED VARIETIES.

Wardwell's Dwarf Kidney Wax Bean—One of the leading varieties for the market

Merchants write to us for special prices on seeds in large quantities.

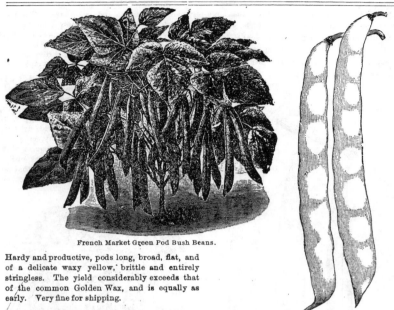

French Market Green Pod Bush Beans.

Hardy and productive, pods long, broad, flat, and of a delicate waxy yellow, brittle and entirely stringless. The yield considerably exceeds that of the common Golden Wax, and is equally as early. Very fine for shipping.

Grenell's Rust-proof Golden Wax.—Vine a little more upright than the Golden Wax, and the waxy-white pods are more nearly straight and proportionately broader than those of that fine variety. A very popular sort with gardeners.

Violet Flageolet Wax—Known also as "Perfection Wax." Plant very large, with large, light green leaves. Pods very long and large, be-

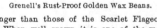

Grenell's Rust-Proof Golden Wax Beans.

ing longer than those of the Scarlet Flageolet Wax. When well grown it is one of the most showy of wax beans. The pods are a little later in coming into use than the Scarlet Flageolet. It is well adapted to the south.

Davis Kidney Wax—This is the most hardy and productive bush wax-podded bean in cultivation. All of the pods are very long, white, straight and handsome. The vine is rustless and vigorous, bearing near the center many clusters, some of which extend above the foliage. When young, the pods are very brittle, crisp and tender. One of the best for shipping and of the greatest value for either the market or home garden.

Prolific Black Wax—The old standard Black Wax bush bean. It is so good that it is worthy of special notice. The pods are round, brittle, of handsome golden yellow color, and of buttery flavor when cooked. Do not forget the old meritorious kind when looking over the list, and include this in your orders.

Detroit Wax—The very hardy, productive, erect growing plants bear their pods near the center of the vine, but occasionally throw a stem above the leaves. Leaves large, dark green; blossoms small, white; pods straight, flat, but thick

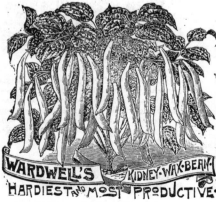

WARDWELL'S KIDNEY WAX BEAN. HARDIEST AND MOST PRODUCTIVE.

Buy our Seeds once and you will buy them all the time.

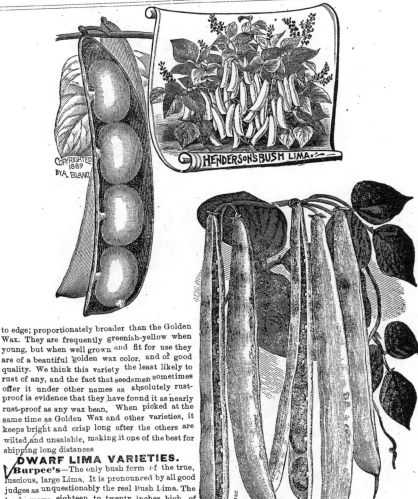

COPYRIGHTED 1889 BY A. BLANC

HENDERSON'S BUSH LIMA.

Violet Flageolet Bush Wax Bean.

to edge; proportionately broader than the Golden Wax. They are frequently greenish-yellow when young, but when well grown and fit for use they are of a beautiful golden wax color, and of good quality. We think this variety the least likely to rust of any, and the fact that seedsmen sometimes offer it under other names as absolutely rust-proof is evidence that they have found it as nearly rust-proof as any wax bean, When picked at the same time as Golden Wax and other varieties, it keeps bright and crisp long after the others are wilted and unsalable, making it one of the best for shipping long distances

DWARF LIMA VARIETIES.

Burpee's—The only bush form of the true, luscious, large Lima. It is pronounced by all good judges as unquestionably the real Bush Lima. The bush grows eighteen to twenty inches high, of stout growth and always erect. It is an immense yielder, the pods being filled with very large beans. Does not do as well here as the Henderson's Bush Lima.

Henderson's—This bush Butter Bean is similar to the small Sieva pole bean. It is the original bush form of the pole beans.—It is the most productive of any, and on the whole is a vegetable of great merit. Is extensively grown here for our home market.

POLE OR RUNNING BEANS.
Culture.

Lima Beans should not be planted before the ground has become warm in spring. Strong poles ought to be set in the ground from four to six feet apart, and the ground drawn around them before the seed is planted. It is always best to plant after a rain and with the eye of the bean down. The other Pole or Snap Beans can be planted flat, and not more than three to four feet apart, and hilled after they are up. Do not cover the seeds more than two inches; one inch is enough for the Southern Prolific and Crease Back.

Southern Prolific—A very prolific sort and popular in the South for snaps. Vines vigorous, with large, thin, smooth leaves; blossoms white; pods produced in clusters, green, cylindrical, or thicker than broad, long, fleshy, crisp; beans small, oval, dun-colored, and somewhat variable in shade.

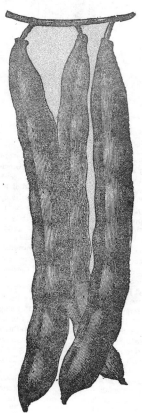

Southern Prolific Pole Bean.   White Creaseback Pole Bean.

Give our Seeds a Trial and be convinced that what we say are facts.

Lazy Wife—The pods are produced in great abundance and measure from 6 to 8 inches in length; they are broad, thick, very fleshy and entirely stringless. The pods retain their rich, tender and stringless qualities until nearly ripe and are unsurpassed in all stages. Each pod contains 6 to 8 round, white Beans, which make excellent Winter shell Beans. They are late to mature, but are valuable to extend the season. This is an excellent Bean and is sure to give satisfaction.

White Creaseback—This variety is especially valuable for its extreme earliness and its habit of perfecting all of its pods at the same time. Vines small to medium, but vigorous, and in good soil wonderfully productive, bearing pods in clusters of from four to twelve. Pods medium length, round, with crease in back, silvery green, of the best quality as snaps, and stand shipping better than most sorts.

Dutch Case Knife — Vines moderately vigorous, climbing well, but twining more loosely than some, and so may be used for a corn hill bean. Leaves large, crumpled; blossoms white; pods very long, flat, irregular, green, but becoming creamy-white; beans broad, kidney-shaped, flat, clear white, and of excellent quality.

POLE LIMA BEANS.

Small White Lima, Carolina, or **Sieva.** — Vines vigorous, with many short branches, so that they are sometimes grown without poles; very early and productive, with small, smooth, dark green leaves and small, yellowish-white blossoms; pods short, curved, thin flat; beans white, small, kidney-shaped.

Large White Lima—Too late for the extreme north, and is being supplanted by Seibert's Early Lima Bean, because the latter is earlier. Vine tall growing, vigorous, but slender; leaves medium sized, smooth, light green; blossoms small, white; pods borne in clusters, long, broad, very thin, dark green; beans large, ovoid, kidney-shaped, greenish-white, flat.

Seibert's Early Lima Bean—One of the finest large Limas ever introduced. The vine is so productive that, although the pods rarely contain more than four beans, the yield is enormous, and is produced from the very first to the last of the season. The green-shelled beans are of immense size, and are tender and succulent.

In earliness, ease of shelling, size, beauty and quality of the green beans, this variety is far in advance of all other sorts.

It is recognized as the best of all the Limas for either the garden or market. Give it a trial.

Early Golden Cluster Wax—A well known, early and very beautiful sort. Vines large,

strong growing, vigorous, hardy; le flets large, light green, crimped; flowers yellowish-white; pods six to eight inches long, borne in abundant clusters, each containing from three to six pods; these are broad, very thick and fleshy, deeply creased along the edge to which the beans are attached and much curved; color bright golden yellow. Of the very best quality, and staying in condition for use a long time. The beans are also excellent shelled green. We recommend this variety as furnishing the largest and handsomest pods of any sort in the list.

Golden Wax Flageolet—It is the best Wax Pole Bean in cultivation, surpassing in length and delicacy of flavor all other Wax varieties. It is a very strong grower, which is wanting by most of the Wax Pole kinds. It bears abundantly, is entirely stringless, and does not spot, even by too much rain or other untoward weather. Cannot be too highly recommended.

BEET.
Culture.

The ground for beets should be rich and well spaded or plowed. Sow in drills twelve to eighteen inches apart, over the seed about one inch deep. When about a month old, thin them out to four or six inches apart. In this latitude beets are sown from January till the end of April, and from the middle of July till the middle of November; in fact, some market gardeners sow them every month in the year. In the summer and fall it is well to soak the seeds over night and roll in plaster before sowing.

Four of the best varieties of Beets. Detroit Dark Red, Improved Egyptian, Eclipse and Edmands Early Blood Turnip.

Schindler's Seeds always grow and give entire satisfaction.

Crosby's Egyptian — SELECTED STOCK. The earliest Beet in the market. A selection from that standard market Beet, Early Egyptian, which retains the earliness of the parent stock and has added thickness, giving it a more desirable shape; it is the deepest red, almost black in color, and is of finer quality than the Egyptian, being sweeter and even more tender and smoother. The most desirable sort for small beets for early market, as it is in presentable shape quicker than any of the others. It is a very rapid grower.

Early Eclipse—Tops small, dark purplish-green shading to lighter color on outside of leaves. Roots nearly globular, with small tap root and very small collar. Flesh dark red, zoned with a lighter shade, very sweet, crisp and tender, especially when young.

Improved Early Egyptian—The best variety for forcing and excellent for first early crop out of doors, being very early, with small

chindler's Crescent City.

top. Leaf stems and veins dark red; leaf dark green, dotted with red; roots very dark red, rounded on top, but flat beneath with very small tap roots; flesh dark red zoned with lighter shade, hard, crisp and tender when young, but becoming woody with age. Our seed is a special selection of the darkest, earliest and most perfect roots with small tops.

Schindler's Crescent City--This is one of the finest strain of Extra Early beets ever introduced and has become the market gardeners favorite for the home market, as well as for shipping. The color is dark red and it is of fine quality, not stringy and much sweeter than most other kinds. Leaf dark green, mottled with red and

deep red ribs; has only one small tap root and no side shoots. Recommend them highly and are worthy of a trial.

Detroit Dark Red Turnip—A grand beet for bunching for market; tops exceptionally small and upright; roots are perfect turnip shape with small tap roots. Color of skin dark blood red. Quality is of the very best, sweet, tender and lasting. One of the best for the market gardener and the home garden.

Edmand's Early Blood Turnip — The roots are of good form, round, with only one single small tap root; the flesh is of a deep blood red color, and very sweet and tender. They can be planted very closely, as they do not grow large and coarse, and have a very small top. It is one of the best for the market gardener and for table use.

Improved Early Blood Turnip—An extra selected stock of blood turnip, having larger, coarser tops and roots than the Detroit Dark Red, and requiring a considerably longer time to mature. Excellent for summer and autumn use.

Silver Beet or Swiss Chard — This variety is cultivated for its large succulent leaves, which are used for the same purposes as Spinach. It is very popular in the New Orleans market.

BEETS FOR STOCK FEED.

Mangel Wurzel Beet—LONG RED. A large, long variety grown for stock feeding. It stands up well above the surface; color light red; flesh white and rose colored.

French White Sugar, Red Top--This is the sort most largely grown for stock feeding in Europe, where the superior feeding value of the sugar beets over the coarse Mangel Wurzel is generally recognized. This sort is so rich in sugar that it is sometimes grown for sugar factories. We do not recommend it for this purpose, but do as a most profitable crop for feeding stock. The numerous green leaves are quite erect and the elongated, egg-shaped root is tinged with red at the top. It is very hardy and productive, yielding about twenty tons to the acre.

BROCCOLI.

Although originating from a very distinct type, the modern improved sorts of Broccoli can scarcely be distinguished from cauliflower; the points of difference being that they are generally taller and the heads more divided. The culture is the same as that given for cauliflower.

Early Large White French—The best variety. Heads white, very compact and hard, continuing firm for a long time. | A hardy, vigorous, easily grown sort.

BRUSSELS SPROUTS.

Brussels Sprouts.

Improved Half Dwarf — The plants, which are very hardy, grow two or three feet high, and produce from the sides of the stalk numerous little sprouts which resemble very small cabbages, one or two inches in diameter. The leaves should be broken down in the fall, to give the little heads more room to grow. They should be treated in all respects like winter cabbage or kale. We offer a carefully grown strain, very hardy, and giving compact round sprouts of large size and good quality.

BORECOLE OR CURLED KALE.

Dwarf German Greens—A vegetable highly esteemed in the northern part of Europe, but very little cultivated in this country. It requires frost to make it good for the table. Treated the same as cabbage.

CABBAGE.

For several years Cabbage Seed has been a leading specialty with us. Our Cabbage Seeds are all grown from approved stock seeds. There is none more reliable, none that can be more implicitly depended upon to give planters uniformly satisfactory results.

Culture.

The requisites for complete success are: First, good seed; this plant is largely dependent upon the best seeds for its success; no satisfactory results can possibly be obtained from poor stock. Second, rich, well prepared ground. Third, frequent and thorough cultivation. A heavy, moist and rich loam is most suitable. It should be highly manured and worked deep. Cabbage is sown here almost every month of the year, but

the seed for the main crop should be sown from July to September. Some sow earlier, but July is time enough. For a succession, seed can be sown till November. The main crop for Spring should be sown from end of October to end of November. The raising of Cabbage for Spring has become quite an item of late years. Stein's Early Flat Dutch, Superior Flat Dutch, Brunswick, Crescent City and Succession should be sown a little earlier than the Early Summer—the latter kind not till November, but in a frame, so the young plants can be protected against cold weather, which we generally have between December and January. After the middle of January setting out can be commenced with. These early varieties of Cabbage require special fertilizing to have them large. Early varieties are sown during the winter and early spring. Cabbage is a very important crop, and one of the best paying for the market gardener. It requires more work and attention than most people are willing to give, to raise Cabbage plants during the months of July and August. The most successful gardeners in raising cabbage plants sow the seeds thinly in seed beds, and water several times during the day; in fact the seed bed is never allowed to get dry from the sowing of seed till large enough to transplant. There is no danger in doing this, of scalding the plants, as many would suppose; but, on the contrary, the plants thrive well, and so treated, will be less liable to be attacked by cabbage flies, as they are too often disturbed during the day. Hammond's Slug Shot and Tobacco dust scattered between the plants and in the walks between the beds is a preventative against the fly and worms.

FIRST EARLY CABBAGES.

Early Jersey Wakefield—The earliest and hardest heading of extra early cabbages. Best

Charleston. or Large Wakefield Cabbage.

Do not buy cheap and spurious seeds as it is only a loss of time and money.

for home garden for extra early crop. Our Stock is grown and selected with the greatest care, and there is none-better, and there are few as good. Heads conical, very compact, solid and of excellent quality. The thick, stout leaves and compact habit make it the best for Early Spring planting.

Charleston, or Large Wakefield—A strain of Wakefield in which the plant is larger, and a little later, the head larger and not so pointed. On account of the fine, solid heads of this variety it is deservedly very popular with market gardeners and shippers to follow the Jersey Wakefield, which is only a few days earlier than this splendid variety.

Schindler's Extra Early Flat Dutch—The earliest flat headed variety. A wonderfully compact plant, with few outer leaves, so that a great number of fine, solid heads can be produced on an acre. Although it does not come to full maturity as early as Jersey Wakefield, it becomes solid enough for use about as early, and is by far the best early sort for those markets that demand a large, round or flat cabbage. The plant is vigorous, with short stem. The leaves are large, broad, and of peculiar light green color. The heads are oval, and very large for the size of the plant, nearly equaling those of the later kinds. Splendid for Spring crop.

Early York—Heads small, heart-shaped, firm and tender; of very erect and dwarf habit, so that they may be grown fifteen or eighteen inches apart.

Early Large York—Succeeds the Early York. It is of larger size, about ten days later, more robust and bears the head better.

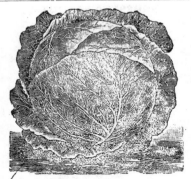
Stein's Early Flat Dutch Cabbage.

Early Winningstadt—One of the best for general use, being very hardy and sure to head, forming a hard head when most sorts fail. Those who have failed with other kinds can hope to succeed with this. It seems to suffer less from the cabbage worm than any other sort. Plant very compact. with short, thick leaves. Heads regular, conical, very hard and keep well both summer and winter. It is the hardiest, not only as regards frost, but will suffer less from excessive wet, drought, insects or disease, than any other second early sort, and will give a fair crop of heads when others fail.

All Seasons — This is the sort generally grown on Long I-land for the New York market. Heads very large, round, often nearly spherical, but usually somewhat flattened; very solid and of

Succession Cabbage.

Schindler & Co's Seeds are the Gardeners Choice.

Crescent City Flat Dutch Cabbage.

the best quality, keeping as well as the winter sorts. Plants very vigorous and sure heading; leaves large, smooth, with dense bloom. Remarkable for ability to stand the hot sun and dry weather.

Large Flat Brunswick—This certainly is one of the very best second early sorts in cultivation, particularly for the home garden. Plants have very short stems and large leaves, which start from the stem horizontally, but turn upward about the head. Head large, very flat, compact and solid, and of fine quality. We have taken pains to have our stock free from the longer stemmed, coarse plants, often seen in inferior stocks of this variety.

Improved Early Summer—This cabbage is not quite so large as the Brunswick; for fall it can be sown in August; for Spring, in November and as late as January. It heads up very uniform and does not produce many outside leaves. It is hardier than the Brunswick and stands the cold and heat better.

Stein's Early Flat Dutch Cabbage. This is one of the earliest cabbages for its size. It is a sure header, very regular and well adapted for shipping. It is planted, exclusive of all other kinds, by some of the largest cabbage growers in this vicinity. One of the best varieties if sown in September and October for an early Spring crop.

Crescent City Flat Dutch——The largest and best of the late market sorts. A strain of Late Flat Dutch Cabbage in which the plants are very vigorous and hardy. The leaves are very large and broad; the stem of moderate height; the head large and very solid. A hardy and very sure heading sort. Always forms a large, handsome head, which keeps better than most sorts. Particularly desirable for those who wish to raise large quantities of cabbage for winter crop. Two weeks earlier than Superior Flat Dutch.

Frotscher's Superior Large Late Flat Dutch Cabbage—This variety is sown by almost all the largest cabbage growers in this vicinity for a winter and late spring crop. It makes a large, solid head and keeps longer in the field without bursting than any other kind. The strain of seed we offer is grown from the old original stock, by one of the most responsible growers in Long Island, and we guarantee none better can be had. This is almost the only variety used by the large truckers in this vicinity for their first sowing in July and August.

Frotscher's Superior Large Late Flat Dutch Cabbage.

Purity, Quality and Reliability ' our motto."

Hollander, or Danish Ball Head Cabbage.

Large Late American Drumhead—
A specially selected strain of this standard variety
for the main crop. It is productive and of best
quality, and finds a ready sale. Almost similar to
Superior Flat Dutch.

Henderson's Success on — This sort
produces large, round, flattened heads which are
of uniform size, very hard and of fine texture, and
weigh from 10 to 15 pounds. It is a good keeper
and shipper, of fine quality and certain to head,
even in the most unfavorable seasons. A general
favorite with gardeners and large growers. It is a
splendid cabbage for sowing in October, for a
Spring crop. Our strain of seed cannot be excelled.

Mammoth Rock Red—This is the best
largest heading red cabbage ever introduced, and
much better than the stock offered as Red Drumhead. No one should plant the latter as long as
our strain of Mammoth Rock Red can be obtained.
The plant is large, with numerous spreading
leaves. The head is large, round, very solid and
of deep red color. Ninety-eight per cent. of the
plants will form extra fine heads.

Hollander, OR Danish Ball Head—
This is one of the best for growing for distant
markets or for late spring use. The plant is vigorous, rather compact-growing, with a longer stem
than most American sorts and exceedingly hardy,
not only in resisting cold, but also dry weather;
it matures its head a little later than the Flat
Dutch. The leaves are large, very thick, bluish-
green covered with whitish-bloom. The head is
round, of less diameter than that of the Flat
Dutch, but very solid. The leaves of the head are
very thick, white and tender and not only overlap
or pass by each other more than those of most
sorts, but are so tightly drawn as to form an exceedingly solid head, which stands shipment better and arrives at its destination in more attractive

shape than those of any other late sort. In quality it is one of the best, being very white, crisp
and tender.

Improved American Savoy—The best
of all the Savoys, either for home use or the
market, and surest to head. The heads are larger,
more solid and in every way better than sorts
called Perfection, Green Globe or Drumhead Savoy. The plants are vigorous, very sure heading
and even more densely and uniformly curled than
the Early Dwarf Ulm Savoy; the heads are globular and of the very best quality.

CARROTS.
Culture.

Requires a sandy loam, well manured the previous year, and deeply spaded up. Should be sown
in drills ten to twelve inches apart, so the plants
can be worked after they are up. Gardeners here
generally sow them broad-cast, and often the
roots are small from being crowded too much together.

Oxheart Carrots.

Early Scarlet Horn—A short, stumpy
variety of medium size, very early and of fine
flavor. Good for family garden.

Early Half Long Scarlet French—
POINTED ROOTED. Excellent for early market, or
for field culture. Of medium size, flesh bright
scarlet, brittle and of fine flavor.

Chantenay — Tops medium size; necks
small; roots tapering slightly but uniformly stump
rooted and smooth; color deep orange-red; flesh
very crisp and tender. Although this is a medium
early sort, it furnishes roots of useable size as early
as any, is a heavy cropper and is undoubtedly one
of the best for both the market and private garden,
while its great productiveness makes it very desirable as a field sort.

St. Valery—This is the most popular variety
with the market gardeners and shippers in this
vicinity. It is bright red in color, a little thicker,
and longer than the Half Long French. It is one
of the finest carrots for the market, as well as the
family garden.

Convince yourself by trying Schindler's Seeds.

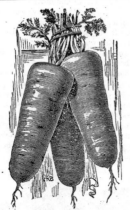

Chantenay Half Long Carrot.

Danvers—Grown largely on account of its great productiveness and adaptability to all classes of soil. Tops medium sized, coarsely divided. The smooth and handsome roots are deep orange, of medium length, tapering uniformly to a blunt point; flesh sweet, crisp, tender and of a deep orange color. This is a popular field variety, and although the roots are shorter, they produce as large a bulk as the longer field sorts, and are more easily harvested.

Improved Long Orange—The most popular of the older sorts for farm use on mellow soil. An improvement obtained by years of care-

St. Valery Carrot.

Improved Long Orange Carrot.

Early Scarlet Horn Carrot.

ful selection of the best formed and deepest colored roots of the old Long Orange. Roots comparatively shorter than the Long Orange, and smoother, but so uniform and true that the bulk of the crop will be greater.

CAULIFLOWER.

The Cauliflower, although one of the most delicious vegetables, is but little grown except by pro. fessional gardeners, because of the erroneous notion that it is so difficult to grow that only skilled gardeners can produce it. Anyone will be reasonable certain of success with this most desirable vegetable if he carefully follows the cultural directions given below:

Culture.

The soil for Cauliflower should be like that for cabbage, but it is better if made richer than is ordinarily used for that crop, giving a rich pasture or clover field the preference. A stiong loam, neither too clayey nor too sandy, is best. Plenty of good manure, horse manure being considered best, must be well incorporated with the soil, and the latter be brought into the highest state of tilth. No application, however, can be more necessary or more useful than that of cultivator and hoe. For late crop sow at same time as for late cabbage, and treat in the same manner.

The Italian varieties should be sown from April till July; the latter month and June is the best time to sow the Early Giant. During July, August, September and October, the Le Normands, Half Early Paris and Erfurt can be sown, but in this section the Algiers has the preference and is considered the best of All.

For spring crop the Italian kinds do not answer, but the Algiers and Half Early Paris can be sown at the end of December and during January, in a bed protected from frost, and may be transplanted into the open ground during February and as late as March. If we have a favorable season, and not too dry, they will be very fine; but if the heat sets in soon, the flowers will not attain the same size as those obtained from seeds sown in fall, and which head during December and January.

Half Early Paris — A most excellent French variety, with good sized, uniform, close heads, which are tender and delicious. Splendid for market gardeners.

Extra Early Dwarf Erfurt—Similar in all respects to "Early Snowball," and nearly as early. It will give excellent results either in the home garden or for market use.

Early Italian Giant Cauliflower.

Early Italian Giant—A distinct and valuable late variety. The heads are very large, extremely white, firm and compact, and being well protected by foliage, remain a long time fit for use. The plants should be started and transplanted early in the season to insure their full development.

Schindler's Early Snowball Cauliflower.

Beware of Tomato Seed obtained from canneries.

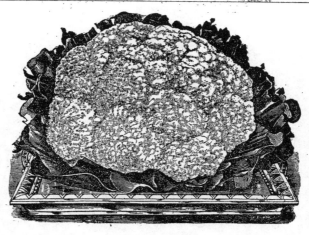

Large Algiers Cauliflower.

Schindler's Early Snowball—An extra Early variety, that forms exceedingly large, compact, round, very white and curd-like heads which are developed earlier than any other variety. Very good sort for planting for late Spring crop, if sown in December and January in cold frames. The seed we offer of this variety cannot be excelled for purity and quality.

Large Algiers.—A valuable late sort, sure to head, of the best quality and very popular with market gardeners everywhere. Plant is large, but of upright growth, the leaves protecting the heads so that they will endure uninjured a frost that would ruin other sorts. One of the very best of the late kinds.

Le Normand's Short Stem—Plant hardy, compact growing, sure heading, and producing many leaves, which protect the close, solid curd, keeping it well blanched. Stands more heat than most other kinds.

CELERY.

Culture.

Sow in May and June for early transplanting, and in August and September for a later crop. Sow thinly and shade during the hot months. When the plants are six inches high, transplant into trenches about four inches deep, nine wide and two and half feet apart, made very rich by digging in rotten manure. Plants should be from 6 to 8 inches apart. When planted out during the hot months, the trenches require to be shaded, which is generally done by spreading cotton cloth over them; latanniers will answer the same purpose. Celery requires plenty of moisture, and watering with soapsuds, or liquid manure, will benefit the plants a great deal. When tall enough, it should be banked up with earth from both sides in order to bleach it for the market.

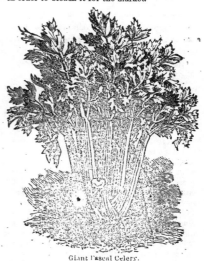

Giant Pascal Celery.

Golden Yellow Large Solid, or **Golden Self-Blanching**—This is the best celery for early use. Critical gardeners depend up-

Give our Seeds a Trial and be convinced that what we say are facts.

CELERY.

Dwarf	White	Perfection	White	Golden
Large Ribbed.	Plume.	Heartwell.	Solid.	Self Blanching.

on our stock of this sort to produce their finest early celery. Plants of a yellowish-green color, but as they mature the inner stems and leaves turn a beautiful golden yellow, which adds much to their attractiveness and makes the work of blanching much easier. The handsome color, crispness, tenderness, freedom from stringiness and fine nutty flavor of this variety make it only necessary to be tried in order to establish it as the standard of excellence as an early sort.

White Plume—While we are fully aware that this variety has great merit as an early market sort, being as early as any, and very attractive when fit for use, yet we do not think that it compares favorably with the Golden Yellow Solid, either in flavor or solidity, or that it will remain in condition for use as long after it is earthed up. Plants light yellowish-green, with tips of leaves almost white, and require to be earthed up but a short time before they are in condition for use. Where a fine appearing celery at a minimum amount of labor is the object, this variety will give entire satisfaction. An *Improved* WhitePlume with longer stems is being offered, but careful comparison with our stock shows that it is not equal in quality or so desirable as that we offer.

Perfection Heartwell—A fine flavored, crisp and tender variety. The stalks are medium sized, round, very solid, crisp, tender, white and of exceedingly fine and nutty flavor. Excellent for market as well as family garden.

Dwarf Large-Ribbed OR **Kalamazoo**—Dwarf, white, stiff variety, close habit, solid and crisp; of fine quality; ribs unusually large and broad.

Giant Pascal—This is a green leaved variety developed from the Golden Yellow Large Solid, and is an excellent sort for fall and winter use. It blanches very quickly to a beautiful yellowish-white color, is very solid and crisp and of a fine nutty flavor. The stalks grow broad and thick, a single plant making a large bunch. With rich soil and high culture this variety will be wholly satisfactory.

Large White Solid—A large sized, vigorous growing variety; stalks white, round, very crisp; perfectly solid and of superior flavor.

Soup, OR **Cutting Celery**—This variety is adapted to sowing thick in rows and cutting when three or four inches high, to use for soup flavoring. It can be cut repeatedly and will furnish a succession throughout the season.

Celery Seed for Flavoring—Oz., 5c; ¼ lb., 15c; lb., 40c.

Schindler & Co's Seeds are the Gardeners Choice.

CELERIAC.
OR TURNIP-ROOTED CELERY.
Culture.

Sow the seed at the same season and give the same treatment as common celery. Transplant the young plants to moist, rich soil, in rows two feet apart and six inches apart in the row. Give thorough culture. As the roots are the edible portion of this vegetable, it is not necessary to earth up or "handle" it. After the roots have attained a diameter of two inches or over, they will be fit for use.

Turnip Rooted Celery.

The root of this celery is turnip-shaped and tender, having a sweeter taste and stronger flavor than other varieties. It is used principally for seasoning meats and soups. If boiled like potatoes, peeled, sliced and seasoned like potato salad, makes a delicious dish when cold.

CHERVIL.

An annual for flavoring; resembles parsley, but the foliage is much smaller and finer; has a strong aromatic taste and is used extensively here for flavoring and seasoning soups, especially oyster soup; also gives a pleasant taste when used in lettuce salad. Should be sown broadcast in fall for winter and spring cutting, and in January and February for summer use.

COLLARDS.

Georgia, Southern or **Creole**—A cabbage-like plant which forms a large, loose, open head, or a mass of leaves on a tall-stem. Freezing does not injure, but rather improves its quality. Sow thick in drills, in rich ground, transplanting when four inches high, or sow in drills where the plants are to remain, and thin to two or three feet apart in the row, when of proper size. In the south sow from January to May and August to October.

CORN SALAD.

This small salad is used during the winter and early spring months as a substitute for lettuce. It should be sown broadcast in drills nine inches apart during fall and winter.

CHIVES.

Chives are very hardy and perennial members of the onion family. They are grown exclusively for their tops. Planted in clumps in any garden soil, they grow rapidly, and increase so as to render a division necessary. The tops appear very early in spring and can be cut throughout the season.

CRESS.

Is used as a salad in winter and spring; it is generally sown in the fall and early spring, broadcast or in drills six inches apart.

Gray Seeded Early Winter—A variety that does well on upland and produces a large cluster of leaves quite similar to those of the Water Cress in appearance and quality. It is quite hardy and thrives best in the cool autumn months.

True Water—This is quite a distinct variety of Cress with small oval leaves, and only thrives when its roots and stems are submerged in water. It is one of the most delicious of small salads and should be planted wherever a suitable place can be found.

Schindler's Seeds always grow and give entire satisfaction.

SELECTED SEED CORN
For Market and Field Culture of the Finest Quality.

The Farmer and Planter can never exercise too much care in the selection of seed corn for planting; as over half that sold in the various stores is nothing more than the ordinary quality for feeding purposes, but possibly better screened. We have made Seed Corn one of our specialties and send out samples which are perfect in both their appearance and growth, and will venture to say that there is no brand of seed corn more sought after than ours. In husking we select the finest and purest ears, and when thoroughly dry take off the small points before shelling; our samples are then thoroughly tested to insure growth, this continued selection has increased both the size of the ear and grain of every variety of seed corn we sell.

Culture.

A rich, warm, alluvial soil is best, but excellent corn can be raised on any good, ordinary soil if it is deeply and thoroughly worked before planting. Plant in hills about three feet apart, drop four or five grains and thin out to two or three. Give frequent and thorough but shallow cultivation until tassels appear; plant for a succession from February to June.

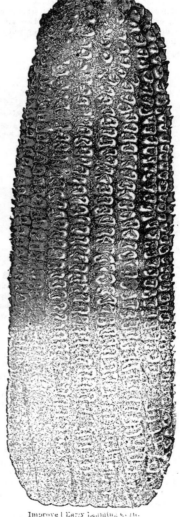

Early French Market.

Adams Extra Early Corn—This is one of the earliest varieties and is only planted by the

Improved Early Leaming Corn.

Do not buy cheap and spurious seeds as it is only a loss of time and money.

Schindler's White Snowflake

duces large sized and well filled ears and comes into market about two weeks later than Extra Early Adams.

White St. Charles Corn—It is a little later than Champion White Pearl, but makes a fine crop for a late market corn; it produces very large, well filled and heavy ears and stands drought better than any other variety.

Champion White Pearl—This is one of the best late varieties for market; it is very productive and produces large, uniform and well filled ears of small grain and pure white. It is planted extensively here for the market.

Improved Early Leaming. The Leaming is the earliest Yellow Dent Corn in cultivation ripening in from ninety to one hundred days from the time of planting; its extreme earliness, productiveness and fine quality has made it very popular with the farmers, and especially with those in the localities where the seasons are short. It is not hard and flinty like most yellow corn, but sweet and nutritious and makes excellent feed and meal. Ears large, with deep, large grains and well covered by the shuck.

Improved Early Golden Dent.--The great advantage of the Improved Golden Dent over all other varieties is for its earliness, productiveness, beautiful ears, deep grain, small cob, and for the superior quality of the meal it makes, It was introduced by us a few years ago. It is not quite as productive a variety as the Chester County Gourd, but we regard it as far superior. It is earlier, requires less strength of ground, and makes a fine quality of golden meal. Those who desire to plant the best field corn should select it; the grains are very deep, cobs very thin and will shell more to a given weight of corn on the cob than any other variety.

Schindler's White Snowflake Corn. This is considered one of the best white field varieties ever introduced in the South. It is far superior to any other and is especially adapted for this section. The stalks grow from seven to eight feet and produce two good size ears each; the cob of which is very small and grains deep. It is a splendid corn for shelling and of fine quality for roasting ears. Makes a first class meal.

Early French Market—Of recent introduction; it has become very popular with our market gardeners, as it is very early and productive, maturing about ten days later than Large Adams. It produces large, fine, small-grained, well-filled ears. It is one of the best early corns ever introduced and is worthy of a trial.

Stowell's Evergreen Sugar — This standard main crop variety excels all other sorts in sweetness and productiveness. It is a fine corn

market gardener here for the first corn for market; but it produces very small ears and is unsalable when the Second early varieties come in.

Large Early Adams—This is one of the leading varieties planted for our market, as it pro-for family use; in fact the best; the only fault with this kind when grown here is that the worms attack it before any other kinds and often ruin the crop.

Hickory King—This is the *largest grained* and *smallest cobbed-corn* ever introduced. It produces from two to four ears to the stalk and makes splendid corn for roasting ears as well as for stock.

Yellow Creole Corn, (Genuine). This is one of the best varieties of yellow field corn for growing a general crop in the Southern States. It stands the heat and drought better than any other variety, (excepting the Mexican June) ever introduced; it makes a fine large well-filled ear and is weevil-proof. It is splendid for stock, is also fine for roasting ears and makes a fine meal, having a flinty grain. It matures in about 90 days.

Mexican June Corn. (Pure).—A white variety of recent introduction; it is a native of the arid regions of Mexico and therefore stands our summer heat and droughts, better than any other corn grown. It is prolific and the stalks produce an abundance of fodder. Has become very popular with the large Planters in Louisiana for late planting. Makes fine roasting ears for a late market

Schindler's Improved White Spine.

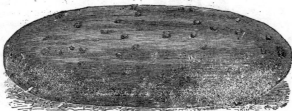

New Orleans Market.

CUCUMBER.
Culture.

Cucumbers need a rich soil. Plant in hills from three to four feet apart; the hills should be made rich with well decomposed manure, and eight to ten seeds should be planted in each hill, and covered about one half inch deep; when well up, thin out to four plants in the hill till the vines meet. When the spring is dry the plants have to be watered, else do not keep in bearing long. They can be planted from March till July. A great many Cucumbers are planted here in February, or even sooner, and are protected by small boxes with a pane of glass on top. These boxes are re-moved during the day and put back in the evening. When days are cloudy and cold, the plants are kept covered. In case of lice making appearance, use tobacco dust or Slug Shot.

Schindler's Improved White Spine—This is an improvement over all other White Spines. The fruits are almost cylindrical in form, slightly pointed at the ends and handsome in appearance, being perfectly smooth and not ridged as in other strains. The vines are of vigorous growth and enormously productive. The fruits retain their dark green color longer than any other variety of White Spine.

Schindler's Seeds are always Pure and Reliable.

Long Green Turkey.

New Orleans Market—This is one of the leading cucumbers planted by the market gardeners for market as well as for shipping; in fact it is the only kind used by the local shippers, if they can be had. It produces fruit from **6 to** 10 inches and sometimes 14 inches long, of a dark green color which it retains longer than any other sort. In shape it is round and tapers at one end.

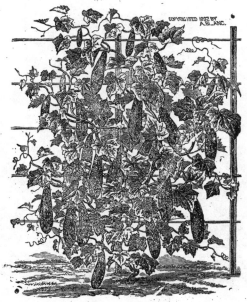

Japanese Climbing.

Merchants write to us for special prices on seeds in large quantities.

The stock of seed we offer is grown from selected stock; none better to be had.

Early Cluster—Early, short and prickly; it bears in clusters.

Prolific Pickling—A slim and slender pickle, from 3 to 5 inches long, covered with black hairy spines. The fruits are of the deepest, green, which, combined with its brittle crispness renders it an ideal pickle. When in the pickling stage the cucumbers show no sign of seed.

Long Green Turkey—A long variety attaining a length of from fifteen to eighteen inches when well grown. Very fine and productive.

Japanese Climbing—While all cucumbers are running vines, yet this variety is much more creeping, or climbing in its habit, so much so that it quickly climbs on poles or trellises in the same manner as the Pole Lima bean. It is entirely distinct. The quality is splendid. It is well adapted for pickling, as well as for slicing for salads. The great advantage of having a cucumber which can be trained on a pole or a fence will be apparent to all. Fine for family garden. Where space is an object; it is quite an acquisition:

Prolific Pickling.

West India Gherkin—This is an oval variety, small in size. When grown to its full size it can be stewed with meat. In fact, this is the only use made of it about New Orleans.

EGG PLANT.
Culture.

The seed should be sown in hot-beds in the early part of January. When a couple of inches high they should be transplanted into another frame, so that the plants may become strong and robust. When warm enough generally during March, the plants can be planted in the open ground, about two and a half feet apart. This vegetable is very profitable in the south, and extensively cultivated.

New York Market Egg Plant.

Schindler's Seeds are the best.   Give them a trial.

New Orleans Market Egg Plant.

New Orleans Market—This is the market-gardeners' favorite and is almost exclusively grown here for the local market and for shipping purposes. It produces. fruit of a large size, oval in shape and dark purple in color, also very productive. It is preferable to any other variety, as it stands our summer heat better and is always a sure cropper and a good shipper, as it seldom rots.

New York Market—A fine sort for shipping. Plants of strong growth with large foliage and in rich soil, productive; the fruit is of large size with smooth and glossy deep purple skin. It is splendid for a general crop.

ENDIVE.

Culture.

A salad plant which is very popular and much cultivated for the market, principally for summer use. It can be sown in drills a foot apart, and when the plants are well up, thinned out till about eight inches apart. Or it can be sown broadcast thinly and transplanted the same as lettuce. When the leaves are large enough, say about eight inches long, tie them up for blanching, to make them fit for the table. This can only be done in dry weather, otherwise the leaves are apt to rot.

For summer use do not sow before the end of March, as if sown soon r, the plants will run into seed very early. Sow for a succession during the spring and summer months. For winter use sow in September and October.

Green Curled—Is the most desirable kind, as it stands more heat than the other sorts, and is the favorite market variety.

Broadleaved Batavian or **Escarolle**—Used as a salad. This is grown quite extensively here of late for shipping, as it carries better than any other variety.

GARLIC.

This is a vegetable which is used to a great extent in the South, especially in Louisiana. It is used mostly by the foreign population, to flavor stews, roasts and various other dishes; also eaten by the Italians with bread and salt. In the past few years it has come into demand more than any other culinary ingredient. It grows splendidly here in our State and produces fine heads, and is largely cultivated, inspite of the fact that large quantities are imported here from Spain and Italy. It is cultivated like onions; should be planted in October and November in drills two to

Truck-Farmers write to us for special prices on large quantities.

GARLIC.

three feet and about six inches in the drill and about an inch deep. In the Spring they are taken up and plaided together in a string by the tops. These strings are made to contain 50 heads and are then hung up in a dry airy place to cure, after which they are shipped to market.

KOHL-RABI, OR TURNIP ROOTED CABBAGE.

Culture.

This vegetable is very popular with the European population of this city, and largely cultivated here. It is used for soups, or prepared in the same manner as Cauliflower. For late fall and winter use it should be sown from the end of July till the middle of October; for spring use, during January and February. When the young plants are one month old transplant them in rows

Vienna Kohl-Rabi.

one foot apart, and about the same distance in the rows. They also grow finely if sown broad-cast and thinned out.

Early White Vienna--This is the finest variety grown for market and shipping purposes; it makes a large sized bulb or tuber and medium sized leaves and does not get stringy as quickly as other kinds; therefore is preferable. Can also be used to grow under glass or in hot-beds. If troubled with flies or lice use tobacco dust or Slug Shot. Our strain is the finest that can be grown.

LEEK.
Culture.

Belongs to the onion family. Sow the seed and care for the young plants as for onions, but they need more room in order to develop fully. When the young plant is about the size of a goose quill, transplant to a prepared bed in rows one foot apart and four or five inches in the row. Set the roots deep, and draw the earth to them when cultivating, so that they may be well blanched by the time they are fit for use.

London Flag—This is the variety generally cultivated in this country. It is hardy and of good quality.

Monstrous Carentan--The largest variety, often three inches in diameter, and becoming very white and tender. A hardy and desirable sort.

Large American Flag—A variety which has become very popular with some market gardeners on account of its being larger than the London Flag.

Monstrous Carentan Leek.

Schindler & Co's Seeds are the Gardeners' Choice.

Large Rouen—Stem very large but comparatively short; the leaf is very broad, covered with whitish bloom. Stands a long time in condition for use.

LETTUCE.

Culture.

There is no vegetable which is more universally used than this, and yet, comparativ.ly few people ever eat really *good* lettuce, as that obtainable in the market is generally of the poorer but more show varieties, and so wilted as to be inferior to well grown heads of the better sorts, fresh and crisp from the garden. We earnestly urge all of our readers who can do so, to grow their own lettuce, and use some of the following varieties.

Lettuce is sown here during the whole year by the market gardener. Of course it takes a great deal of labor to produce this vegetable during our hot summer months, and the following instructions should be followed:

Before sowing, soak the seeds for half an hour in water, take them out and put in a piece of cloth and place in cool spot—under the cistern, or if convenient in an ice box. Keep the cloth moist, and in two or three days the seeds will sprout. Then sow them. It is best to do so in the evening, and give a good watering.

The richer and better the ground the larger the head will be. No finer lettuce is grown anywhere else than in New Orleans during fall and spring. The seed should be sown broad-cast, when large enough, planted out in rows a foot apart and from eight to ten inches apart in rows.

Improved Royal Cabbage — This is a popular variety. Heads light green, of large size, and about two weeks later than the White Butter. It is very tender and crisp; can be sown later in the spring than the foregoing kind and does not run into seed so quickly.

Schindler's Early Market — This is one of the best varieties for an all season Lettuce; as it grows very quickly and produces large fine heads with a golden yellow heart and seldom goes to seed as other kinds do.

New Orleans Improved Passion Lettuce.

Trocadero—This is a beautiful light green Lettuce and forms large, solid, tender heads, with few outside leaves, which are inclined to curl. It is the leading variety planted by the market gardeners and truckers here for shipping in the winter and spring; it is also very hardy. Our stock of seed cannot be surpassed for its fine heading quality.

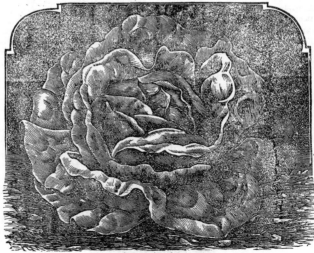

Schindler's Early Market Lettuce.

If you want to make a success in gardening, use Schindler's Seeds.

New Orleans Improved Passion— A strong growing sort with large green leaves, marked with scattered brown dashes. It forms a very solid head of rich, creamy yellow leaves, which are very thick, tender and of splendid quality. This sort is very hardy and is extensively grown in winter for shipping and early market use.

Paris White Cos, or Roman Lettuce.

Big Boston—(Seed White.) A very popular variety with those gardeners who want a large heading, forcing sort, and also for outdoor winter culture. The plants are large, very hardy and vigorous, with broad, comparatively smooth, thin and very hard leaves which are bright, light green in color, and when well grown are quite tender. Indoors this forms a solid head, while outside it is less distinctively a heading sort. This, is grown in the south as a winter lettuce.

Paris White Cos or Roman—The Cos lettuce differs entirely in shape from the other varieties, the head being elongated and of conical form, eight or nine inches in height, and five or

six inches in diameter. The outer coloring of this variety is yellowish-green. To be had in perfection it requires to be tied up to insure bleaching. Used here extensively by the French and Italian population; splendid for table use.

Early White Butterhead—Plants medium sized, with numerous round, smooth leaves which are of a beautiful yellow color, and very sweet and tender. They form medium sized, fairly solid heads which, when prepared for the table, are exceedingly attractive in appearance.

Brown Dutch—An old sort noted for its hardiness. Leaves large, thick, green, tinged with brown. It always forms a large, solid head which is somewhat coarse looking, but the inner leaves are beautifully blanched, exceedingly sweet, tender and well flavored. Desirable because of its hardiness and fine quality.

MUSK MELON.
Culture.

Cultivate as recommended for cucumbers, except that the hills should be six feet apart. Rich earth for the young plants is far better than manure, but if the latter must be used, see that it is well rotted and thoroughly mixed with the soil. If the plants grow very rank, more and finer fruit will be secured by pinching off the ends of the shoots when they are about three feet long. The quality of melons of all varieties is largely dependent upon conditions of growth and ripening. Unhealthy vines or unfavorable weather produces fruit of comparatively poor flavor.

Rocky Ford—This new musk melon is similar to the oval strain of Netted Gem. The strain here offered originated with the melon growers in the vicinity of Rocky Ford, Colorado, who have shipped this melon from that distant western point to eastern markets. The melons

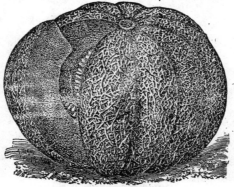

New Orleans Market Musk Melon.

Do you want to make a success in gardening? If so, buy your seeds from us.

grown by them are so fine in quality as to outsell all others, and the demand for such melons has been far beyond the supply.

Chicago Market—Fruit large, round or slightly oval with very shallow depressions and covered with dense netting. Flesh green, medium texture, very thick and sweet, The variety is an improvement on Montreal and will suit those who like a large, sweet, green-fleshed sort.

Netted Nutmeg—Small oval melon, roughly netted, very early and of fine flavor.

Early White Japan—Early sort of creamish white color, very sweet and of medium good variety for shipping.

Osage Musk Melon—Cultivated extensively for shipping North; it is of small size and smooth skin, but is very attractive and deliciously sweet. Splendid for family use.

Netted Citron—This is a medium sized melon, round in shape and roughly netted. Very sweet and musky in flavor.

Emerald Gem Melon — The Emerald Gem is entirely unlike any other musk melon yet introduced. The melons are about the size of the Netted Gem, but, unlike that variety, the skin, while ribbed, is perfectly smooth, and of a very deep emerald green color. The flesh, which is thicker than any other native melon of the same size, is of a suffused salmon color, and ripens thoroughly to the thin green rind, which is distinctly defined. The flesh is peculiarly crystaline in appearance, and so very juicy, sweet and rich that it almost drops to pieces. It matures very early, and is quite productive.

New Orleans Market—One of the best melons that can be grown in the South for shipping as well as family use. Of extra large size, sometimes averaging 16 pounds; very sweet and of high flavor. It is roughly netted and of greyish green color; grown here extensively for this market; in fact the only melon raised in this section.

WATER MELON.

Culture.

In order to get good Water Melons it is essential that the plants get a good start, and to this end it is important to prepare hills about eight feet apart, by thoroughly working into the soil an abundance of well rotted manure, and in this plant the seed as soon as the ground becomes warm and dry. Frequent watering of the young plants with liquid manure will hasten their growth and help them get out of the way of insect pests.

Georgia Rattlesnake—One of the oldest and most popular sorts, particularly in the South. Fruit cylindrical, square at the ends, smooth, distinctly striped and mottled light and dark green. Flesh bright scarlet and very sweet.

Kolbs Gem — Vines of medium size, but remarkably vigorous and healthy, Leaves of medium size, deeply cut with a peculiar frilled edge. Fruit of the largest size, round or slightly oval, marked with irregular mottled stripes of dark and light green. Outer rind or shell exceedingly hard and firm, making it a good sort for shipping long distances. Flesh bright red, solid, a little coarse, but sweet and tender.

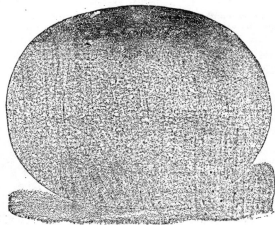

Kolbs Gem Water Melon.

Schindler's Seeds are the best for Purity and Quality.

Dixie Water Melon.

Dixie—A popular market sort Vine vigorous, large growing and hardy; fruit medium sized to large, about one-third longer than thick. Color of skin dark green, striped with a lighter shade; rind thin but tough; flesh bright scarlet, ripens closely to the rind, is of the best quality and free from the hard, coarse center which is so objectionable a feature of many shipping melons.

Ice Cream—The old but extremely popular home market melon. There is none better, nor a more handsome melon grown. It is medium in size, almost round; the skin a pale green, slightly mottled; flesh bright scarlet, fine-grained, solid to the center, sweet, crisp and melting. Its delicious flavor entitles it to the name.

Sweet Heart Water Melon—This new melon is early, large, handsome, heavy and productive. The shape is oval, and color mottled light to very light green. Flesh bright red, solid, but tender and very sweet. We have a very fine stock grown from selected stock seed procured from the originator, hence it is as pure and true as the original.

Triumph—A southern variety which has become very popular with shippers. The fruit is uniformly large, nearly round, dark green, indistinctly striped with a lighter shade; rind thin and

Triumph Watermelon

Our Seeds are Fresh, Reliable and True to Name.

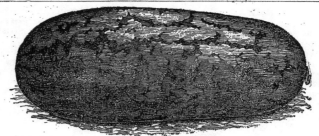

Florida Favorite Water Melon.

firm, making it an excellent shipper; flesh bright red and of good quality.

Florida Favorite—A very large, long melon, mottled dark green, with stripes of lighter shade. Rind thin but firm; flesh very bright, deep red; very sweet, tender and excellent. A very popular variety in the South. One of the finest melons for family use.

McIvers Wonderful Sugar Melon—The sweetest melon grown. Without a single exception this is the sweetest water melon of all. The melons attain a great weight, are of a very handsome appearance, never crack or lose their fine flavor in the wettest season. It is a very productive and hardy variety, and one that will take the lead wherever known.

Lone Star Water Melon—This is one of the finest varieties of water melons ever introduced and cannot be excelled for its fine quality in solidity, crispness and sweetness. It is long and uniform in shape, rind light green in color, marked with dark mottled stripes. One of the best for market as well as family use.

MUSTARD.
Culture.

This is grown to quite an extent in the Southern States, and is sown broadcast during fall, winter and spring. It may be used the same as Spinach or boiled with meat as greens. The White or Yellow Seeded is very little cultivated, and is used chiefly for medical purposes, or pickling. The large-leaved or Curled has black seed, a distinct kind from the Northern or European variety. The seed is raised in Louisiana. It makes very large leaves; grown extensively by the market gardeners in this vicinity.

Large Leaved Curled—This is the favorite kind here, sown largely for the market. Leaves are pale green, large and curled or scalloped on the edges.

Chinese Very Large Cabbage Leave — This is a European variety, with light green very large leaves. It has not the same taste as the large-leaved or the large curled, but will stand longer before going to seed.

NASTURTIUM.
Culture.

Sow early in spring in drills one inch deep or, if for ornament, in boxes near a trellis, fence or some other support to climb upon. They thrive very well in any kind of soil.

Dwarf Nasturtium.

Tall Nasturtium—This is cultivated a great deal in the South for its foliage and beautiful flowers, but is also grown for its berry like seeds, which are gathered when green and put in vinegar and are then called capers, which are frequently used here for seasoning and flavoring stews and meats.

Dwarf Nasturtium—Same as above, but dwarf in growth and used mostly for ornament.

Schindler's Seeds are the best.

OKRA.

This is one of the most popular vegetables grown in the South and is being cultivated on a larger scale every year. It is used in making the celebrated dish known as CREOLE GUMBO. It is also boiled in salt water and, when cooled off, mixed with vinegar, sweet oil and other seasoning and served as a salad. It is wholesome and nutritious, also a healthy vegetable for the stomach.

Early French Market Okra.

Culture.

Should be planted early in spring or as soon as the ground is warm, as, if sown too early, the seed will rot. Sow in drills two to three feet apart, and when the plants are up, thin out. leaving one or two plants every twelve or fifteen inches in the row.

Tall Growing—This is a good variety for the market, but since the dwarf sorts have been introduced it is not being cultivated to any large extent.

Early French Market—This is one of the best sorts for market as well as for family use, and is almost exclusively used here by truckers and market gardeners. It is of a half dwarf growth and very prolific; the pods are of a light green color, seldom ribbed, and remain tender much longer than any other kind.

White Velvet—This is a white Okra, dwarf, with long, round, smooth pods, free from ridges. Fine for family use.

ONIONS.

Culture.

In Onion culture, thorough preparation of the soil, careful sowing and the best of culture, though essential for a good yield, will avail nothing unless seed of the best quality is used. With the same care and conditions, Creole onion seeds grown in two different sections may be so unequal in quality of good, merchantable onions that it is more profitable to sow only the purest and best stocks. Our Seed is grown by a reliable grower on Bayou Lafourche, and only the choicest bulbs are set out for the growing of our seed. We do not depend on chance purchases, as some houses do; as many times some unscrupulous trucker will cut seed from shot-up onions which are utterly unfit to grow merchantable stock for the market. The onion crop is one of the leading vegetables planted for our market, for shipping as well as home use. Thousands of barrels are grown in the State of Louisiana and are shipped to the leading cities in the United States in the spring and early summer. The only and best keeping sort for our section and other neighboring States is the Creole Onion. Under favorable circumstances—that is, if our spring season is not too wet—the Red and White Bermuda seed (Teneriffe grown) will make a fine onion, but not as good a keeper as the Creole,

and is much milder in flavor. The proper time to sow the seed is after the 15th of September. It also can be sown in January and February, thinly in drills.

Creole, or Louisiana—This variety is of brownish red color and very solid; it is of fine flavor and half round in shape. It is a longer keeper than any Northern or Western sort and seldom gets soft.

Red Bermuda—(Teneriffe grown.) This is a splendid sort for early shipping and for bunching for market. Red in color and flat in shape; grow to very large size in rich soil. Fine for family use and home market.

White Bermuda — (Teneriffe grown.) Same as the Red variety, but pure white in color and mild in flavor.

White Queen—(Italian.) This is of medium size, very early and flat in shape; can be sown as late as February and still good-sized bulbs will be had. It is mild in flavor and is splendid when boiled and served with white sauce for table.

SHALLOTS.

A species of small onion which is used in its green state for flavoring soups, stews, salads, etc. It grows in clumps, which are divided and set out in the fall of the year and early spring in rows a foot apart and about six inches in the rows. Latter part of spring, when the tops are dry, they are taken up, thoroughly dried and spread out thinly in a dry, airy place.

Truck-Farmers write to us for special prices on large quantities.

White Queen Onion..

ONION SETS.

Onion Sets, when planted in January and February here in the South, will most always produce fine large bulbs. They should be set out in rows five to six inches apart and about eight or ten inches in the rows.

Red Western Sets—Will produce a fairly good onion, but are planted mostly for use in the South as green onions. They do very well in North Louisiana and Mississippi.

Creole Sets—These are the best for this section and will produce good sized bulbs under favorable conditions, and make good, solid onions and long keepers.

Yellow Western Sets—Same as the red sets, only different in color, which is of a pale yellow or brown.

White Western Sets—A fine variety of same quality as the red and yellow sets, but are not as hardy and do not keep as well.

Schindler's Seeds are the most reliable.

PARSNIP.

The value of the Parsnip as a culinary vegetable is well known, but is not generally appreciated at its full value for stock feeding. On favorable soil it yields an immense crop of roots, which are more nutritious than carrots or turnips, and particularly valuable for dairy stock.

Culture.

They do best on a deep, rich, sandy soil, but will make good roots on any soil which is deep, mellow and moderately rich. Fresh manure is apt to make the roots coarse and ill-shaped. As the seed is sometimes slow to germinate, it should be sown as early as possible, in drills two feet to two and one-half feet apart; cover one-half inch deep and press the soil firmly over the seed. Give frequent cultivation, and thin the plants to five or six to the foot.

Parsnips.

Hollow Crown, or Guernsey—Root white, very tender, with a smooth, clean skin. The variety is easily distinguished by the leaves growing from a depression on the top or crown of the root.

PARSLEY.

Culture.

Sow in the all from August to November and in the spring from January to May. It is generally sown broad-cast. Used a great deal for seasoning and ornamenting fancy dishes.

Parsley.

Plain Parsley—This is the only variety grown for the New Orleans market; as it grows tall and makes very dark colored leaves; is also stronger in flavor and hardier than the other varieties.

Champion Moss Curled—A compact growing, finely cut and thickly curled sort of a bright green color. Very ornamental for decorating fancy dishes. It is grown here very extensively lately, for shipping to the northern and eastern markets during winter and early spring.

PEAS.

Culture.

For early Peas the ground should be light and well manured the year previous; as fresh manure will produce a rank growth of vine and they will make only a small and uneven crop, at the same time a poor quality of peas. Late Peas, such as the Marrowfats, can be successfully grown in a moderately heavy soil; as, if sown in too rich ground, they will not bear much of a crop. The early varieties can be planted in the months of August, September and October and during January, February and March. The Marrow-fats should be sown in November, December and January for a late crop, as they stand more cold, also bearing longer than the early kind.

Schindler's Extra Early—This is the earliest and best of all the extra early kinds. It has held the lead for many years on the New Or-

Try Schindler's Seeds and you will always want them.

Early Alaska Peas.

leans market, and is yet the best variety for gardeners. It is very prolific and ripens so uniformly
that the vines can be cleaned up at one picking.
This is a desirable feature, as the gardener can
sell his entire crop on a top market. It is the best
variety for all-round purposes.

Early Washington, Early May OR
Frame, which are nearly all the same thing,
are about ten days later than the Extra Early. It
is very productive and keeps longer in bearing

than the foregoing kind. Pods are a little smaller.
Very popular about New Orleans.

Early Alaska—By careful selection and
growing we have developed stock of this smooth,
blue pea, of unequaled evenness of growth of
vine and early maturity of pods. Vines two to
two and one-half feet high bearing four to seven
long pods which are filled with medium ized,
bright green peas of excellent flavor. Ripe peas
small, bluish green Matures all the crop at once

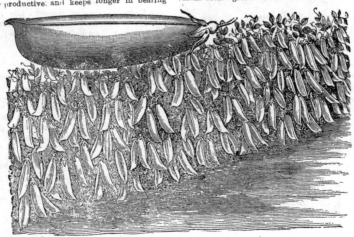

Schindler's Extra Early Peas

Our Peas are grown from the finest stocks and are true to name.

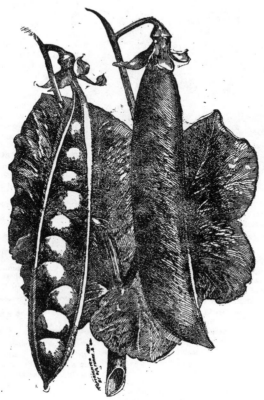

Carter's Stratagem Peas.

and is an invaluable variety for market gardeners and canners.

Extra Early Premium Gem — Seed wrinkled. Vines 14 to 18 inches high, extra early in season; quality very choice; the most productive of the very dwarf varieties; excellent for market.

American Wonder—A variety nearly as early as the First and Best, with stout, branching vines about nine inches high and covered with well filled pods containing seven or eigth large exceedingly sweet, tender and well flavored peas. Dry peas medium sized, much wrinkled, pale green. We have taken great pains in growing our

stock and know it to be much better than that usually offered.

Champion of England (WRINKLED).—green-wrinkled variety, famous for its delicious flavor, it is a shy bearer, consider it one of the finest varieties for family use, and will follow any of the second early varieties in ripening, the germ of this pea is very delicate, and should the weather be wet or damp for several days after planting it will invariably rot in the ground, and another planting should at once be made.

Large White Marrowfat—Cultivated very extensively for the summer crop. Vines about five feet high and of strong growth. Pods large, cylindrical, rough, light colored and well filled; seeds large, smooth, round and yellow or white, according to the soil in which they are grown. It

Purity, Quality and Reliability is our motto.

Early Washington Peas.

is excellent for summer use, but inferior in quality to most of the newer sorts, although undoubtedly one of the most productive of the garden varieties.

Improved Stratagem—Most stocks of the large-podded, semi-dwarf, English varieties of peas have been so wanting in uniformity and evenness of type as to disgust American planters, but by constant effort we have developed a stock of this, the best variety of that class, which comes true, and we do not hesitate to pronounce it one of the best of the large podded sorts. The pods are of immense size and uniformly filled with very large, dark green peas of the finest quality. One of the very best varieties for market gardeners and family use.

First and Best.—This is a strain of Extra Earlies, which when first introduced gained quite a reputation, but within a few years they have been superceded by other varieties which have proved not only much earlier but far more productive; average height of growth three feet, and owing to their strong growth, will continue in a bearing state longer than the finer strain of Extra Earlies.

Telephone (WRINKLED).—A marvelous variety, producing pods of prodigious size and well filled with mammoth peas of exquisite flavor. Growth, five feet; an extra-ordinary cropper.

Blue Beauty.—This is a blue, round pea, which is nearly as early as the famous American Wonder, but far more productive and a sure cropper; the uniform height of its growth is two feet, so regular is its appearance when growing in rows it resembles a miniature Ledge; its pods is of medium size and well filled. Its quality and flavor cannot be surpassed.

Laxton's Alpha (WRINKLED).—Each year adds still more attractive features to this desirable early wrinkled variety; it produces fine, large-sized pods, very productive, and of exquisite flavor, resembling the old Champion of England.

Field, OR **Cow Peas**—Used very extensively here in the South for fertilizing, as well as for making hay for winter feed. It is splendid for fattening hogs, and when the pods are dry and threshed the peas make a splendid feed for poultry. They should be sown from April till July broad-cast; if to be used as a fertilizer. The vines should be plowed under when about two to three feet long. Clay Peas and Whippoorwills are the leading kinds used.

Black-Eyed Marrowfat—An excellent variety, growing about five feet high; pods large; a prolific bearer and can be recommended as one of the best Marrowfat sorts. Very hardy.

HINTS ABOUT PEAS.

The crop should be gathered as fast as it is fit for use. If even a few pods begin to ripen, not only will new pods cease to form but those partly advanced will stop growing. Our Schindler's Extra Early Peas are the money-makers and the only kind to sow for the early market.

PEPPERS.

Culture.

To raise pepper plants successfully and to have them early for market, the seed should be sown in a hot-bed during January, and as soon as the weather moderates and the plants are large enough they should be transplanted into the open ground in rows from 18 to 24 inches apart and about 15 inches in the rows. Never sow sweet peppers in close proximity to the hot varieties; as they will mix readily.

Sweet Spanish Monstrous—This variety is almost exclusively planted by the market gardeners here for our market and for shipping. It is very mild, of a beautiful green color, of large size, tapering towards the end. Superior to any other kinds for salads or stuffed.

Ruby King—A sweet pepper which grows to a very large size; produces fruit from five to six inches long and about four inches in diameter. Is mild in flavor and can be used as a salad same as Sweet Spanish.

Golden Dawn OR **Mango**—Of a beautiful golden yellow color, very attractive, mild and sweet; in shape it resembles the Bull Nose. Fine for family use.

For fresh Seed. True to Name send your orders to us.

Long Red Cayenne Pepper.

Long Red Cayenne—This is a long narrow sort, tapered and inclined to curve; it is very hot and used a great deal in the South for seasoning and making pepper sauce.

Tabasco — (Genuine). Grown extensively for making the well known Tabasco pepper sauce; in fact it is almost the only kind raised for that purpose: it is the hottest variety of the pepper family. It is very prolific, as it produces bushes three to four feet high, which are literally covered with fruit which is about three-quarters to an inch in length and narrow. They are easily gathered, as the peppers do not adhere to the stem, which is quite an advantage over the other kinds.

Sweet Spanish Monstrous Pepper.

Birdeye—A very hot and prolific sort; also attractive and ornamental; the fruit does not get any larger than a small pea and is of a deep red color. Is fine for putting up in bottles with vinegar and used for seasoning purposes.

POTATOES.

Early Triumph Potato.

We make a specialty in handling only the best varieties of *Seed Potatoes* and only offer such kinds which are best adapted to our climate and have been proven by careful tests to be the best producers for this market

The early varieties produce best in light, dry, rich, sandy soil; the best fertilizers, is well rotted stable manure, cotton seed meal or super-phosphates will also answer very well. Always select good size and medium potatoes for Spring planting; cut each tuber to two or three eyes to each piece; plant in drills about three feet apart in or-

Ruby King Pepper.

Schindler's Seeds are the best.

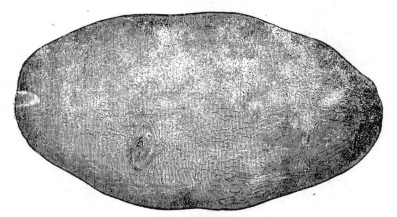

Boston Peerless Potato.

der to cultivate them properly. In planting them in gardens, two feet apart is sufficient. The proper time to plant potatoes is from middle December till later part of March; the best time for a general crop, is to plant from latter part of January to end of February. Potatoes can be also grown successfully here in the South for a Fall crop; the tubers should be planted during August and September. The seed must be planted whole; as if cut, the potatoes are apt to rot; therefore all the small potatoes or cullings should be used from the Spring crop for seed stock.

The best potatoes for this section and vicinity are the Boston Peerless, Early Rose and Early Triumph. The latter do well on Piney Wood land: if fertilizers are properly used We carry the following varieties in stock and consider them the best sorts to plant in the Southern States for earliness and productiveness for the market and family use.

Early Ohio Potato.

Early Rose—The earliest and best potato for family use and for shipping to distant markets. It is quite productive and does well on light, rich soil. The potato has a light pink skin; is oval and long, flesh pure white and very mealy when boiled

Early Triumph—This variety has become very popular and is extensively grown; on light, sandy soil and piney wood land, where it produces prolific crops of good sized tubers. It is of a fine round shape, light red color, flesh pure white and excellent for table use. Our stock of seed is genuine second crop Tennessee grown. None better to be had.

Early Ohio.—A seeding of the Rose, resembling in color, of round-oblong shape: it is of fine quality, about a week earlier than the Rose, is a good yielder, and one of the very finest varieties for the table.

Early Beauty of Hebron Potato.

Boston Peerless—One of the leading kinds for our market and is almost exclusively planted by the gardeners and truckers in this vicinity.

Schindler's Seeds are the Market Gardeners favorite.

Early Rose Potato.

Early Beauty of Hebron.—One of the best of the early varieties. In some sections it proves earlier than the Early Rose vine vigorous, growing very rapidly; very productive. Tubers similar in shape to the Early Rose, but shorter. Skin tinged with link at first, but becomes pure white during the Winter. It is of the finest quality.

PUMPKINS.

Mammoth Tours Pumpkin.

Culture.

Pumpkins can be grown in almost any kind of soil; of course the richer the ground the larger fruit they will produce. They should be planted in hills 10 to 12 feet apart and cultivated same as melons or cucumbers.

Large Cheese. OR **Field**—Most popular sort for field and market use; splendid for feeding cattle. It is of large, round, flat shape, salmon-yellow in color, solid and a long keeper. Used to quite an extent in the outh for table use.

Large Cheese or Field Pumpkin.

Cashaw Crook-Neck—(Greenstriped. This is the leading variety planted for the New Orleans market. It is of a greenish-yellow color with deep green stripes; flesh is fine grained, yellow and sweet. Best kind for table use.

Cashaw Crook-Neck Pumpkin.

Mammoth Tours Pumpkin. —This variety is famous for the size of the Pumpkins it produces; which frequently weigh from 100 to 125 lbs. It is of a grayish yellow color, flesh is coarse grained and fine for stock-feeding. Where size is an object, we recommend this variety.

RADISH.

Early Scarlet Turnip (White Tipped) Radish.

Culture.

Radishes are grown here for our markets all the year around on an extensive scale. The ground should be well prepared, rich and mellow; the

We supply two-thirds of the New Orleans Market Gardeners with our Seed.

early varieties can be sown broad-cast, amongst other crops, as Spinach, Carrots, Lettuce. Beets and Peas. During the summer months in order to have the radishes to mature quickly and be brittle, they have to be watered frequently The leading varieties used here are the Half-Long Scarlet French; Long Brightest Scarlet and White Strasburg. During the winter the Early Scarlet Turnip White-Tipped is sown largely for shipping to the Northern markets.

Half Long Deep Scarlet Radish.

Long Black Spanish—One of the latest as well as the hardiest of radishes; an excellent sort for winter use. Roots oblong, black; of very large size and firm texture.

mp. Long Scarlet Short Top Radish.

Early Scarlet Turnip—(White-Tipped.) One of the handsomest of the turnip radishes and a great favorite in many large markets for early planting out-doors. It is but little later than the White-Tipped, Forcing and will give entire satisfaction where extreme earliness and small top are not the primary objects Ro ts slightly flattened on the under side; color very deep scarlet with a white tip: flesh white and of the best quality Planted extensivly by the Market gardeners here for shipping to the N rthern markets.

Long Brightest Scarlet, White-Tipped—This is the brightest and handsomest colored, scarlet radish known, and a decided improvement in ear iness and color over other varieties of this class. It makes roots fit for use in about twenty-tive days from time of planting, and they continue in good condition until they are full grown, when they are as large as the Wood's Early Frame. It has a small top, and does not ru_ to neck

Improved Chartier Radish

Half Long Deep Scarlet—The roots of this hardy and desirable variety are of a very brilliant, deep, rich red color, and half long with a somewhat taper ng point; the fle h is very white, crisp and tender, and holds ts juiceness v ell, not becoming pithy till overgrown.

Early Long Scarlet. Short Top Improved—This small topped sort is about six inches long grows half out of the groud, and is a standard and excellent sort either for private gardens or market use. It continues brittle and tender until July. The roots are very uniform in shape, smooth, and very bright red in color. The flesh is white and crisp.

Market Gardeners always give our Seeds the preference.

Long Black Spanish Radish.

is one of the most salable varieties, as its very attractive appearance always insures its sale.

Early White Box—This is one of the very best varieties for either forcing, cold frame culture, or for early sowing in the open ground. They are of the most perfect form, of a paper-white color, very mild, of pleasant flavor and exceedingly early.

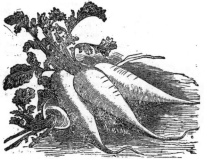

White Summer Strasburg Radish.

White Summer Strasburg—This is a very desirable early summer variety, of an oblong tapering shape and of pure white color, is exceedingly crisp and tender; it forms its roots very quickly, and can be sown throughout the Summer, as it stands the heat remarkably well; it is a very popular variety in our markets and is rapidly becoming one of our most salable varieties here.

Chartier—This radish is quite distinct in appearance from any other variety; it is long like the Long Scarlet; the color at the top is crimson, running into pink about the middle; the balance of the root downward is pure white. It will grow to a large size before it becomes pithy.

White Strasburg—This grows to the largest size, and is usable when quite small, thus covering a long season. The mature roots are four to five inches long and about two inches thick, very white; the flesh is exceedingly crisp and tender. One of the best of the large summer varieties.

Yellow Summer, Turnip Rooted—Very symmetrical and uniform; nearly round, with grayish-white skin, covered with a bright yellow russeting, which makes it very attractive. The flesh is compact, white, and rather pungent.

Long White Vienna, or Lady Finger—A very excellent white variety with long very smooth, white roots, which are crisp and tender; it is one of the most desirable of the white summer sorts.

Early Scarlet Globe—This very beautiful German variety has proved a very great favorite; it is of a brilliant scarlet color, of globe shape, short leaved and very early; remarkable, not only for its great beauty and its extreme earliness, but

Salsify.

SALSIFY, OR VEGETABLE OYSTER.

The long, white, tapering root of Salsify resembles a small parsnip, and when cooked is a good substitute for oysters, having a very similar flavor. It is fine when grated and made into batter cakes and patties.

Culture.

It succeeds best in a light, well enriched soil, which should be spaded or plowed very deep. It should be sown during the beginning of September, not later than December. Sow in drills about 8 to 10 inches apart, and thin out 3 to 4 inches in the row.

Mammoth Sandwich Island—This is the only kind planted here, as it is superior to the common variety, being larger, growing stronger and not liable to branch.

SORREL.

Culture.

This is a vegetable which will grow almost in any kind of soil, rich or barren, and will last for three or four years. It is used mostly for soups and salads; also cooked like Spinach.

Large Leaved French—The best garden variety; produces large, pale green leaves of fine quality.

SPINACH.

Spinach is very hardy, extremely wholesome and palatable and makes a delicious dish of greens retaining its bright green color after cooking. It is also pronounced one of the healthiest vegetable grown.

Culture.

Plant in very rich ground; the richer, the larger the leaves. Sow during the fall from September until March, broad-cast or in drills one foot apart.

Broad Leaved Flanders Spinach.

Broad-Leaved Flanders—One of the most vigorous and strong growing varieties. The leaves are nearly round, uniformly bright green, quite thick and slightly crimped in the center. One of the best sorts for our market and for shipping.

Large Leaved Savoy—This is an early variety; produces narrow pointed leaves, curled like those of the Savoy cabbage; only good for family use; goes to seed quickly in spring.

SQUASH.

The squash is one of the most nutritious and valuable of all our vegetables. Few farmers recognize the value of winter squashes, costing no more than an acre of corn to cultivate and easier gathered, will give as much food available for feeding stock as corn will.

Early White Bush or Patty Pan Squash.

Culture.

For first and early crop the seed of squash should be planted in boxes beginning of February, but the best time is to sow them when the ground gets warm and danger of frost is over. Sow during March for a general crop in bills from three to four feet apart, 6 to 8 seeds in a hill; when well up thin out to three or four of the strongest plants.

Early White Bush or Patty Pan—This is a beautiful clear white variety, uniform in shape, well scalloped, and is superior to any other kind for market.

Yellow Summer Crook-Neck—This is a strong growing variety, very early and productive. Fruit measures from 10 to 15 inches in length, with crooked neck and covered with wart-like excrescences; of bright yellow color and very tender.

Hubbard—This is one of the best winter squashes; flesh of bright orange yellow, fine-grained, very dry, sweet and rich flavored; keeps perfectly throughout the winter and can be used for baking like sweet potatoes; it is splendid for feeding stock.

TOMATOES.

Culture.

Tomatoes do best on light, warm and not over-rich soil; success depends upon securing a rapid, vigorous and unchecked growth during the early part of the season. Sow the seed in January, in hot-beds or in flat boxes placed near a window in a warm room. When the plants are from 3 to 4 inches high they should be transplanted into another hot-bed in order to make them strong and sturdy. When the danger of frosts is over, which is about the middle of March, they should be transplanted into the open ground in rows 3 to 4 feet apart. They should always be supported by stakes or wire supports, as, if allowed to grow

Do you wish to make a success in gardening? If so, buy your seeds from us

Improved Trophy Tomatoes.

wild, the fruit at the bottom of the vine is apt to rot. In March the seed can be sown in the open ground for a general crop. For a late fall crop the seed should be sown from May to August

Favorite—This is one of the leading kinds for our market; it is solid, uniform in shape and of a beautiful rich, dark red color; it is also exceedingly smooth; flesh very firm. Market gardeners' favorite.

Stone—This is the heaviest and most solid fruited of the large tomatoes of good quality. Our stock is superior to any offered under that name. being more uniform, better colored and larger, Vigorous and productive vines, fruit round, apple-shaped, very large, deep red in color and solid.

Beauty—We have been selecting this to a larger, smoother fruit than the original stock, and think we have made it the smoothest and best of the large purple sorts. Vines large, vigorous and heavy bearers; fruit large, uniform in size,

very smooth; color of skin purplish-pink; flesh light pink and of excellent flavor

Acme—We have given a good deal of attention to the improvement of this variety, and think we have succeeded in making it one of the smoothest and most uniform, medium sized early, purple fruited sorts Vines large, hardy, and productive, ripening its first fruit almost as early as any, and continuing to bear abundantly until cut off by frost. Fruit in clusters of four or five, invariably round, smooth and of good size, free from cracks and stands shipment remarkably well; flesh solid and of excellent flavor. For market gardeners who want an early, purple fruited tomato, either for home market or to ship, for private gardens or for canners, it is one of the b st. This variety is used for planting under glass

Improved Trophy—The Trophy was the first of the modern improved sorts, and it had qualities of color, size and solidity hich entitled it to hold a place against the much lauded new

Our Seeds always give utmost satisfaction.

Dwarf Champion Tomato.   Beauty Tomato.

kinds; though all admitted it lacked in smoothness and regularity. By most careful breeding and selection, there has been produced a strain in which all the original good qualities are retained and even more highly developed, yet it compares favorably with any in smoothness, regularity and symmetry of the fruit. We offer our Improved Trophy as a sort whose large, strong growing, vigorous and productive vine, very large, very solid, smooth, fine flavored, and beautiful, deep, rich red fruit will satisfy the most exacting.

Dwarf Champion—This is a purple fruited variety, which forms very stout, strong plants about two feet high. The branches are short, making a bushy plant that stands quite erect without stake. This sort is often sold as

Tree Tomato. Fruit smooth, medium sized, color purplish-pink, fairly solid, but has no hard core, and is of good flavor. About as early as any purple fruited tomato, and is quite popular in some localities, both for market and home use. The dwarf habit of the vines makes it very desirable for forcing, as it can be planted closer to the glass, and more closely on the bench than the tall growing kinds. Our stock is a very superior strain with larger, smoother fruit than the original.

Perfection—This is one of the handsomest tomatoes grown, and all who have tried its invariably large, round, smooth, handsome, red fruit pronounce it of the highest quality. It has been used very satisfactory for forcing under glass.

For fresh Seeds True to Name send your orders to us.

Stone Tomato.

Favorite Tomato.

Beware of Tomato Seed obtained from Canneries.

TURNIPS.

Culture.

Sow in June till November in drills 16 inches apart or broad-cast and covered lightly, in new ground or in land that has been manured and worked in, the year previous. If the ground has been used for other crops for some time, the land should be sprinkled with land plaster and well worked to incorporate same. For a late spring crop they should be sown in January, February and March; when they will do very well for summer use. Ruta Bagas should be sown in drills or ridges, from middle of July to middle of September.

Extra Early Purple Top Milan—The earliest turnip in cultivation—about two weeks earlier than purple top strap-leaved. The root is flat, of medium size, quite smooth with a purple top. Flesh white, hard and of fine quality.

Early White Spring—An early white variety; something similar to the Early White Flat Dutch Turnip, not so large, but of fine quality; best kind to be sown for early Spring crop.

Extra Early Purple Top Milan Turnip.

Early Purple Top (Strap-leaved).—This is an early variety and a great favorite with market gardeners here for an early crop; it is also a fine variety for family use. It is flat in shape, like a broad dish and grows to a good size and very large in rich soil. It is pure white, with a purple or dark red collar, fine grained, white fleshed and sweet; very tender. Leaves few and uprigh in growth; splendid for table use.

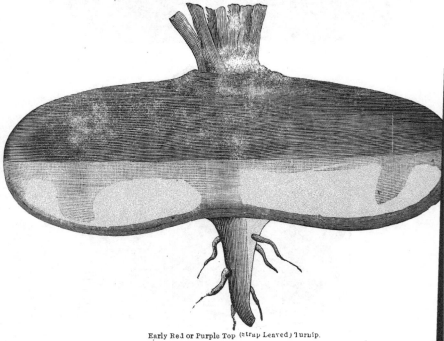

Early Red or Purple Top (strap Leaved) Turnip.

Try Schindler's Seeds and you will want no other.

Early White Flat Dutch Turnip.

Early White Flat Dutch (Strap-leaved.) This is an early kind and is largely planted for the earliest market variety, is similar in shape to the *Purple Top Flat* and also has its good qualities, but is pure white and does not sell well on the market, when the Purple Top sorts come in.

Purple Top Globe—This is the leading Turnip for the New Orleans market for a general crop and is grown extensively by the truckers here. It is of same shape as the White Globe, but has a purple or dark red collar and is beautiful in appearance, of most excellent quality, a strong grower and very hardy. It is a splendid table sort; in fact, none better to be had, as it keeps longer than any other kind, and does not become spongy as the other sorts.

Pomeranean White Globe—This is one of the most productive kinds and in good, rich soil, roots will frequently grow to twelve pounds in weight. It is of perfect globe shape, pure white and smooth. Splendid for table as well as for stock food.

White Egg—A quick-growing sort, very early, egg or oval shaped; pure white, with small top. Flesh very sweet, firm and mild.

Cow-Horn—Is pure white in color, long in shape like a carrot; but crooked; it is inclined to grow half out of the ground. It is of rapid growth, well flavored and is fine for table use as well as for stock food.

White Hanover—This variety resembles the Ruta-Baga in shape and partakes of its nature. The flesh is white, hard, firm and sweet; is a long keeper; fine for table use and is especially recommended for feeding cattle during winter and early spring.

Large Amber Globe—One of the best yellow varieties for a field crop for stock or for table use. Flesh yellow, fine grained and sweet; color of skin yellow, top green. It is hardy and a good keeper; should be planted more for stock food.

Yellow Globe—Almost similar to the above and the roots do not get quite as large; but more globular in shape.

Our Seeds are always Fresh and True to Name.

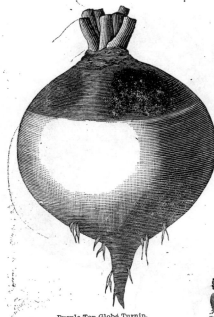

Purple Top Globe Turnip.

The following collections are gotten up for such parties who desire to grow an assortment of vegetables for a family garden at a low figure and also to convince the public that our seeds are what they are represented to be.

FOR 50 CENTS,

we will mail 20 packets as follows:

Beets,	Water Melon,
Cabbage,	Musk Melon,
Carrots,	Mustard,
Celery,	Okra,
Cucumber,	Onion,
Collards,	Sweet Pepper,
Egg Plant,	Parsley,
Endive,	Squash,
Lettuce,	Tomato,
Leek,	Turnip.

Golden Ball—Undoubtedly the most delicate and sweetest yellow-fleshed turnips introduced. It is of medium size; firm, hard and of excellent flavor. One of the best yellow varieties for table use. A good keeper.

Improved Purple Top Ruta Baga. (Long Island Grown).—This is one of the best varieties of Ruta Baga ever introduced; it is very hardy and productive and has very little neck. Uniform in shape, few side roots; flesh yellow, of solid texture, sweet and well flavored; shape slightly oblong, terminating abruptly; color deep purple above and bright yellow under the ground. Leaves small and light green.

Seven Top—This variety is grown mostly in North Louisiana and parts of Mississippi, for the tops, which are used for greens. It is very hardy and grows all winter, but does not produce any eatable roots. Can be used like Spinach or Mustard.

Purple Top Yellow Aberdeen—Produces roots of medium size, round in shape, flesh pale yellow, tender and approaches the Ruta Baga hardiness and texture; it is very productive.

Our 25c. Collection.

We will mail you 10 packets of the following choice vegetable seeds, free of postage:

Beets,	Lettuce,
Carrot,	Mustard,
Cucumber,	Water Melon,
Cabbage.	Egg Plant,
Squash,	Tomato.

Give our Seeds a Trial and be convinced that what we say are facts.

TOBACCO SEED.

Havana Tobacco (Imported.)—We have the genuine strain of the celebrated Vuelto Abajo variety, the leaf of which is only used for the manufacture of the finest cigars in the world. None better to be had. Price, 30 cents per oz.; $4.00 per pound.

Connecticut Seed Leaf Tobacco.

Connecticut Seed Leaf—One of the best American sorts for making cigar wrappers and for pipe smoking. Price 20 cents per oz.; $2.50 per lb.

AROMATIC, MEDICINAL AND POT HERBS.

General Cultural Directions.

Most of the varieties thrive best on sandy soil, and some are stronger and better flavored when grown on that which is rather poor, but in all cases the soil should be carefully prepared and well cultivated, as the young plants are for the most part delicate and easily choked out by weeds. Sow in drills sixteen to eighteen inches apart, taking pains that the soil is fine and pressed firm-ly over the seed. Seeds should be sown early in spring; such varieties as Sage, Rosemary, Lavender and Basil are best sown in a frame and then transplanted into the garden. Most of them should be cut when in bloom, wilted in the sun and thoroughly dried in the shade.

Anise (*Pimpinella anisum*).—A wellknown annual herb whose seeds, which have an agreeable, aromatic odor and taste, are used for dyspepsia and colic, and as a corrective of griping and unpleasant medicines. Sow early and thin to six to ten plants to foot of row.

Balm (*Melissa officinalis*).—A perennial herb, easily propagated by division of the root or from seed The leaves have a fragrant odor, similar to lemons, and are used for making balm tea for use in fevers, and a pleasant beverage called balm wine.

Basil, Sweet (*Ocimum basilicum*.—A hardy annual from the East Indies. The seed and stems have the flavor of cloves, and are used for flavoring soups and sauces.

Borage (*Borago officinalis*).—A hardy annual used as a pot herb and for bee pasturage. The leaves immersed in water give it an agreeable taste and flavor. Sow in beds and thin to six to ten inches apart. In some localities this sows itself and becomes a weed.

Caraway. (*Carum carui*).—Cultivated for its seed, which is used in confectionery, cakes, etc. The leaves are sometimes used in soups. If sown early in August the plants will give a fair crop of seed the next season, but when sown in the spring, will not seed until the next year. Plant in drills two or three feet apart, and thin out if necessary.

Dill (*Anethum graveolens*).—An annual grown for its seeds, as well as for the greens as they both have a strong aromatic odor and a warm, pungent taste. The seed is good for flatulence and colic in infants and the greens are excellent for flavoring pickles.

Fennel (Sweet Florence; *Foeniculum officinalis*. This is grown extensively here by the Italian gardeners for the market, and is also called *Italian celery*. It is used for soups, fish sauces and salads; is also eaten like celery dipped in salt. The seeds are also used for flavoring.

Lavender (*Lavendula vera*).—Hardy, perennial, growing about two feet high. Used for the

Aromatic, Medicinal and Pot Herbs.

Try Schindler's Seeds and be convinced as to their Reliability.

distillation of lavender water, or dried and used to perfume linen. Pick before it becomes dry and hard and dry quickly, so it will retain its odor.

Marjoram; Sweet (*Origanum marjorana*).—A perennial, the young tender tops being used green for flavoring or they may be dried and used for winter for flavoring meats, sausage etc.

Rosemary (*Rosmarinus officinalis*).—Hardy perennial with fragrant odor and warm, aromatic bitter taste. Used for tea.

Rue (*Ruta graveolens*).—A hardy perennial with a peculiar smell. The leaves are bitter, and so acrid as to blister the skin. It is a stimulant and anti-spasmodic, but must be used with great caution, as its use sometimes results in serious injury. It must not be suffered to run to seed, and does best on poor soil.

Sage (*Salvia officinalis*).—A hardy perennial possessing some medicinal properties, but cultivated principally for use as a condiment; it being used more extensively than any other herb for flavoring and dressing. Sow early in spring (four to five pounds per acre in drills) on very rich ground, cultivate often and thin the plants to sixteen inches apart. Cut the leaves and tender shoots just as the plant is coming into flower and dry quickly in the shade. The plants will survive the winter, and may be divided. If this is done they will give a second crop superior in quality.

Summer Savory (*Satureia hortensis*).—A hardy annual, the dried stems, leaves and flowers of which are extensively used for flavoring, particularly in dressings and soups. Culture the same as that of Sweet Marjoram.

Thyme (*Thymus vulgaris*).—This herb is perennial, and is both a medicinal and culinary plant. The young leaves and tops are used for soups, dressing and sauce; a tea is made from the leaves, which in some cases will relieve nervous headache. Sow as early as the ground will permit.

GRASS SEEDS.

Red Top (*Agrostis vulgaris*).—In Pennsylvania and states further south, this is known as *Herd's Grass*, a name applied in New England and New York to Timothy. It is a good, permanent grass, standing our climate well, and makes good pasture when fed close. When sown alone, use about twenty-eight pounds of seed per acre. Sow in spring or fall.

Orchard Grass (*Dactylis glomerata*).—One of the most valuable grasses on account of its quick growth and valuable aftermath. It has a tendency to grow in tufts, and does better if sown with clover, and as it ripens at the same time as clover, the mixed hay is of the best quality. When sown alone, about twenty-eight pounds are required per acre; if sown with clover, half that quantity. It is perennial, and will last for years, but its habit of growth unfits it for lawns.

Kentucky Blue Grass, Fancy Clean *Poa pratensis*).—Sometimes called June grass, but the true June or Wire Grass is much inferior. Kentucky Blue Grass is the most nutritious, hardy and valuable of all northern grasses. In conjunction with White Clover it forms a splendid lawn; for this purpose use not less than 54 lbs. of Blue Grass and six pounds of White Clover per

acre. If sown by itself for meadow or pasturage about twenty-eight pounds per acre will be required. Sow early in the spring, or in October or November.

English or Perennial Rye Grass.

Timothy (*Phleum pratense*).—This is the most valuable of all the grasses for hay, especially in the North. Thrives best on moist, loamy soils of medium tenacity. It should be cut just when the blossom falls. Sow early in the spring or fall, at the rate of twelve pounds per acre; if alone, but less if mixed with other grasses.

English or Perennial Rye Grass (*Lolium perenne*).—A very valuable variety for permanent pasture. Succeeds well on almost any soil, but is particularly adapted to moderately moist or irrigated lands. Sow thirty to forty pounds per acre, in spring.

Meadow Fescue, or English Blue Grass (*Festuca pratensis*).—A perennial grass from two to four feet high, with flat, broad leaves. This is one of the standard European grasses. It needs rich ground, and succeeds well on prairie soil. This is an excellent pasture grass to take the place of the wild grasses, as it yields a large amount of early and late feed. Sow about twenty-five pounds per acre.

Red Clover.

We supply two-thirds of the Market Gardeners trade in New Orleans.

Crimson Clover.

partial shade, forming an excellent cover for the land after the crop is taken off, and will afford a close, dense mat of growing foliage to turn under in the spring. Sow at rate of 15 lbs. to the acre.

Tall Meadow Oat Grass (*Avena elatior*). A hardy perennial much used in the south and west. Its roots penetrate deep, and it thrives on any good soil. It yields a heavy crop, and is valuable both for meadow and pasture. If used alone, sow about thirty to forty pounds per acre.

Bermuda (*Cynodon dactylon*). — No other grass is better known in the south than this variety; it is easily grown from seed and also by sodding. It is splendid for pasturage and is best for making lawns; for this purpose it cannot be excelled, if cut close occasionally; it will grow thick and dense, making a regular carpet. It is superior (for lawns or golf links) to any lawn grass mixture on the market.

Red Clover (*Trifolium pratense*).—This is a fine grass for sowing late in fall, for cutting early in spring and feeding green to stock of all kinds. Can also be sown early in spring for pasture Sow 8 to 10 lbs. to an acre.

White Dutch Clover (*Trifolium repens.*) —Same as the red excepting the flowers are white; generally used for pasturage.

Alfalfa or Lucerne (*Medicago sativa*) — This clover-like plant growing from two to three feet in height. is especially adapted for dry climates and soils. It strongly resembles clover in habit of growth and feed value, but withstands drought much better. It is a perennial plant on well-drained soils, so that when once established it will continue to produce large crops from five to ten years, sometimes longer; on rich high land it produces four to five cuttings in a single season. The plant is quite hardy, but does not succeed well on low, wet soils

Crimson Clover (*Trifolium incarnatum*).— An annual variety providing large crops of green forage, or if cut while in bloom will make excellent hay. It should not be allowed to grow too old, or the seed-heads are liable to cause hairballs to form in the animals' stomachs, to their great injury. It is for use as a green manure and cover crops that this plant is most highly esteemed. It improves poor lands and restores to fertility those worn by excessive culture. Seed should be sown early in August or September, so that the plants will become well established before winter. It is especially valuable for sowing amongst corn or other crops at time of the last cultivation, as it will secure a good stand in the

Alfalfa or Lucerne Clover.

Sainfoin or Esparsette (*Onobrychis sativa*).—This is a very valuable perennial plant for the Southern States; it is quite hardy after it be comes well established. It has strong. deeply branching roots, and will succeed in very dry soils, sand, and even in gravel. Sow 2 to 3 bushels per acre. Bushel weighs about 24 lbs.

Johnson Grass (*Sorghum halapense*).—This grass is popular in some portions of the South and West, being of quick growth, the stouts talks reaching a height of six or eight feet before flowering; should be cut for hay when it is coming into bloom. When once established, it is *difficult to eradicate.* 25 lbs. to the bushel; about 1 bushel to the acre.

Texas Red Rust Proof Oats—This is the only variety of oats which is not liable to rust here in the South. It is one of the most profitable crops that can be grown for winter and spring feeding and will save lots of corn. The seed can be sown beginning of October until latter part of November and again during January and February. They should not be sown as thick as the other kinds, as they have a tendency to stool. Use one and a half bushel to the acre.

Texas Rye—This is sown during the fall months up to January for forage and pasture. During Winter and early spring it also does well if planted thinly with Texas Rust Proof Oats.

Texas Barley—Should be planted in Fall and Winter for forage and is used for feeding, in its green state. It is eagerly eaten by live-stock of all kinds and is very nutritious. Sow on rich soil.

German Millet—This is the favorite variety for planting in good land to produce a large crop of hay or forage during the summer months. Being of very strong growth, the seed should not be sown too thickly; one bushel to the acre.

Velvet Bean—This bean originated in Florida a few years ago, and has become very popular with the farmers and planters in the South. It makes a splendid forage for stock and makes a splendid fertilizer, if turned under like cow-peas. The vine is most rampant in growth, branching freely and growing quickly to a great length; they are thickly clothed with large green leaves. Planted to enrich the soil, they should be allowed to die down, as it is impossible to plow under the dense network of strong vines while in the growing state.

Giant Beggar Weed—This quickly-growing plant is now extensively grown in the Southern States. Sown from beginning of April until June, the seed being small should be simply rolled after sowing broad-cast. Eight to ten lbs. are sufficient for an acre of land; growth is extremely rapid, and the plant may be pastured or cut for forage at any stage, but should be cut for hay before the seed ripens and slowly dried in windrows like clover.

Burr or California Clover—This clover is supposed to come from Chili. It is often mistaken for alfalfa in growth, but is quite distinct in blossom. Burr clover produces 2 to 3 yellow blossoms in each cluster and lucerne has several blue blossoms in an elongated head. It furnishes good grazing and hay. The seeds are produced in burr-like pods and are hard to remove; therefore, they are sown in the burr, half bushel to the acre. Cover the seed lightly and sow in the fall.

DWARF ESSEX RAPE.

Farmers of the United States are just beginning to find out what England has known for many years, that the Fodder Rape is the most valuable green feeding plant known, especially for sheep. Dwarf Essex Rape is easily grown and perfectly hardy, and possesses remarkable fattening properties. One acre will pasture thirty-six head two months and lambs will make a gain of 8 to 12 lbs. a month. *Pigs and Cattle are also very fond of it.* The plant is a rank grower and should have heavy manuring as well as high cultivation. Any corn soil will grow Rape. Sow the seed by the end of June, and the crop can be ready to feed at a *season when it is most needed.* It does well sown with oats. After the oats are cut the Rape grows rapidly. *From ½ acre there were cut 9¾ tons of green rape,* or it yielded at the rate of 19 *tons per acre.* If the soil is rich and clean sow broad-cast; if not so clean, sow in drills and cultivate as for corn. When sown broadcast use 5 lbs., and if in drills, 2 lbs. to the acre. True Dwarf Essex Rape, our own importation.

Australian Salt Bush—A forage plant for alkali soils, and for regions subject to periodic drought. This is a most wonderful forage plant; as it will grow freely in arid and alkali lands, that will produce no other vegetation, yielding a marvelously liberal foliage which is eagerly eaten by all kinds of stock. It is of creeping habit. From twenty to thirty tons of green fodder have been harvested from one acre. It has further been proved that after three or four crops have been grown on alkali land, the soil is then capable of producing any other vegetation. In many sections of the states this is in itself of priceless value. This plant has been very extensively tried at the California experimental station, where single plants, grown on the poorest alkali land, have reached a diameter of sixteen feet in one season. One pound of seed will plant an acre. It grows readily from seed, and requires no cultivation.

VETCHES.

Sand, Winter or Hairy (*Vicia villosa*).—This is the best variety and thrives well on poor soil, especially arid sandy lands. It is best sown in the fall, but does well also if sown early in spring. It grows to a height of from three to four feet and can be cut twice for fodder, first when the blooms appear and then it can be cut for the seed. Very nutritious and hardy. Sow one and one-half bushels to the acre.

Teosinte (*Reana luxurians*).—This is a valuable forage plant resembling Indian Corn in appearance and grows very quickly, producing a large quantity of forage. The leaves are much longer and broader than those of Indian Corn, also more abundant, while the stalks contain a sweeter sap. The forage is exceedingly tender and is greedily eaten by horses, mules and cattle. As it is quite susceptible to cold, the seed should not be sown before latter part of February, beginning of March.

SORCHUM.

Early Amber—This variety is extensively grown here in the South for forage and cutting green when half grown, and makes a splendid fodder for feeding horses, mules and cattle. It is also grown on a small scale for making syrup in such localities in the south where sugar cane does not thrive well.

Early Orange—This sort is almost similar to the Early Amber, but is said to produce more saccharine matter and juice.

KAFFIR-CORN.

This is a variety of Sorghum which grows from four to five feet in height; in habit of growth the plant is low, stocks perfectly erect and foliage wide. It produces an abundance of forage, which horses and cattle are fond of; it also produces a large quantity of seeds which makes splendid feed for fowl of all kind. Requires 10 lbs. to sow an acre.

PEANUTS.

Peanuts can be raised with but little expense, and are an exceedingly productive and paying crop. They are planted in much the same manner as potatoes, and require but little care beyond hilling up the young plants.

Spanish—This is an early variety and very prolific. The pea is smaller than the Virginia and Tennessee; but fills out well, making no pops. Can be planted close in the row and yield largely per acre. Splendid for feeding hogs; also fine for roasting. Should be sown during March, April and May.

White Virginia—This is the original peanut or *pindar*, as it is sometimes called. It is considered the best variety for growing South. Produces pods or shells from 1½ to 2½ inches in length containing from 3 to 5 peas in a pod. Very productive and fine for roasting.

Merchants send in your orders to us; as our seeds always prove satisfactory. Write us for special discount.

SPANISH PEANUTS.

FLOWER SEEDS.

ANNUALS AND OTHER FLOWERS BLOOMING THE FIRST YEAR FROM SEED.

AILANTHUS, OR TREE OF HEAVEN.

AILANTHUS — (Tree of Heaven.)

—This splendid ornamental tree is a native of China, where it is called the Tree of Heaven, from its great beauty. It is very hardy and grows in any soil, no matter how poor and grows from 6 to 10 feet high from seed the first summer. The leaves, from 5 to 6 feet in length, give it a grand appearance. Nothing outside the tropics can rival it for lawn decoration. Large panicles of bloom, followed in season by great clusters of colored seed pods, make the tree a continual thing of beauty. The cut represents a portion of a tree in bloom and also a seedling tree four months from sowing. For beautifying lawns and flower beds nothing can be finer, they being even more beautiful than Ricinus or Cannas. Pkt. 5 cts. Give it a trial.

Abutilon or Bell Flower.

Truck-Farmers write to us for special prices on large quantities.

Snapdragon.

Adonis, Aestivalis, or Flos Adonis—
Has fine, pretty foliage, with bright scarlet flowers. November till April.

Alyssum Maritimum—This is of easiest
culture and its fragrant, pure white flowers which
it bears in clusters bloom almost all summer and
are splendid for making bouquets. Sow October
till March.

Antirhinum Majus — Snapdragon.
Choice mixed. Showy plant of various colors.
About two feet high. Should be sown early, if
perfect flowers are desired. Sow from October
till March.

Aster—German Quilled. Perfect double quilled
flowers, of all shades, from white to dark purple
crimson. One and a half feet high.

Aster—Trufaut's Pæony-Flowered. Large
double pæony-shaped flowers of fine mixed colors;
one of the best varieties Two feet high; sow from
December till March. They can be cultivated in
pots to perfection.

Calleopsis or Correopsis

Amaranthus Caudatus — Love Lies
Bleeding. Long red racemes with blood red flowers. Very graceful, three feet high.

Double Mixed Balsams.   Mixed Canuas.

Our Seeds are Fresh, Reliable and True to Name.

Cosmos

German Quilled Aster.

Abutilon or Bell Flower — These plants are easily grown and bloom profusely during the early spring and summer months. They grow readily from seed and make large fine shrubs, and are beautiful with their bell-shaped flowers.

Althea Rosea (*Hollyhock*). — A beautiful plant growing from 4 to 6 feet high and producing a large number of flowers along the main stem or trunk, of variegated colors. Sow from October till April.

Balsamina Camelia-Flora — Double Mixed Balsams. A free blooming plant of easy culture. The flowers resemble a camelia in form and are of large size. Our mixture contains all the finest variegated colors and cannot be excelled. Sow from February till August.

Balsams, Double White—This is a perfectly double variety and pure white.

Amaranthus Tricolor — Three-colored Amaranth Very showy; cultivated on account of its leaves, which are green, yellow and red. Two to three feet high.

Amaranthus Bicolor — Two-colored Amaranth. Crimson and green variegated foliage; good for edging. Two feet high.

Amaranthus Salicifolius — Fountain plant. Rich colored foliage; very graceful. Five to six feet high. All varieties of Amaranthus should be sown from February to June.

Aquilegia—Columbine. Beautifully, curiously formed, various-tinted flowers. Bloom early in spring and fall. Hardy perennial; sow from October till March.

Ageratum (*Mexicanum*).—Fine plants for masses in the garden for winter and early spring blooming; flowers are brush-like in appearance; remain long in bloom.

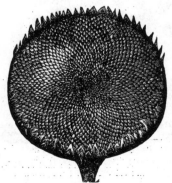

RUSSIAN SUNFLOWER.

If you want to make a success in gardening, use Schindler's Seeds.

Dianthus Hedewigii.

Bellis Perennis—Double Daisy. Easily grown from seed and come into flower in a short time; they are indispensable for spring flowers for the garden. October till February.

Browallia — Handsome plants, eighteen inches tall, with shining green foliage and bright blue and pure white flowers mixed. Sow in February and March. Also in November under glass.

Cacalia Coccinea—Tassel Flower. Small tassel-like blooms, often called "*Flora's Paint Brush*," gracefully borne on long stems. February till May.

German Stocks.

Calendula (*Officinalis*).—Pot Marigold. An aromatic herb; but is mostly planted for its beautiful golden yellow flowers. Sow from January till April.

Calleopsis or Correopsis — Compact plants, covered with bright golden flowers, each marked with dark brown center. Sometimes called *Bright Eye Daisy.* Sow December to April.

Cockscomb (*Celosia cristata*)—Is easily grown from seed, and is certainly one of the most showy and brilliant of annuals. The combs of the varieties grown from our seed often grow a foot or

more across the top. Sow from February till August.

Glasgow Prize—A fine dwarf variety, dark leaves and crimson combs.

Dwarf Mixed—Large solid heads of bloom, red, yellow and variegated colors.

Lobelia Erinus.

Campanula Speculum—Bell-Flower, or Venus' Looking-Glass. Free flowering plants of different colors, from white to dark blue; one foot high. Sow December till March.

Centaurea Cyanus—Bottle pink. A hardy annual of easy culture, of various colors; two feet high.

Margaruite Carnation.

Convince yourself by trying Schindler's Seeds.

Rocket Larkspur.

Large Trimardeau Pansy.

Centaurea Suavolens — Yellow Sweet, Sultan. December to April.

Cineraria Maritima—"Dusty Miller." A handsome border plant, which is cultivated on account of its silvery white leaves. Stands our summer well.

Coleus—A well known and beautiful bedding plant, which can be easily propagated by seeds which produce different shades of colored plants.

Chrysanthemum—Double Mixed. Fine summer bloomers of different colors; they make a fine showing when planted in groups. March to May.

Dwarf Nasturtium.

Schindler's Seeds are the best. Give them a trial.

Large Mixed German Pansies.

Cannas—Finest mixed colors, tall and dwarf.
Sow from February till April.

Tall Nasturtium.

Schindler's Seeds always grow and give entire satisfaction.

Candy-Tuft—White and Purple. Among the most useful of perfectly hardy annuals; produces neat clusters of flowers very freely, which are very fragrant. Sow October till April.

Cosmos—Of very rapid growth and make large bushes, fully 5 to 6 feet high, which are a mass of elegant foliage. From August until November each plant is covered with hundreds of showy blossoms. The flowers resemble single dahlias. They are easily raised and make a grand display. The flowers are of many different colors.

Sweet Violet.

Petunia Hybrida.

Dianthus Chinensis (Double Chinese Pink).—Produces clusters of small double flowers, fine mixed; one foot high. From October to April.

Mixed Phlox.

Buy our Seeds once and you will buy them all the time.

Dianthus Heddewigii—Finest mixed. (Japan Pink). This is a very showy variety. The flowers are large and of brilliant colors; one foot high. Sow October till April.

Dianthus Barbatus (Sweet William).— Of beautiful colors and very showy; should be sown early in order to have them bloom the first spring. One and a half to two feet high. Sow October till April.

Danthus Caryophyllus, Margari-tae.—Marguerite Carnation. These lovely; fragrant Marguerite carnations will bloom in about four months, after sowing the seed. The plants do well in pots, as well as in the open ground and are of vigorous growth and require no support. Eighty per cent produce double flowers and are exquisitely sweet. They are of remarkable colors and shades. Sow November till April.

Delphinium—Larkspur. Well known annuals of great beauty and noted for richness of colors.

Double Dwarf Rocket—Finest mixed. Tall Rocket. Double mixed.

Dahlia—Double; large flowering. The double dahlia can be grown easily from seed and produces fine flowers the first year. The seed should be sown from February till June.

Escholtzia (California poppy.) — Mixed flowers. Flowers yellow, orange and white; leaves very finely cut; grows 10 to 12 inches; very showy. December till April.

Gaillardia.—This plant produces flowers of magnificent size and wonderful profusion, and are greatly admired for their fine forms and rich blending colors. Sow January till April.

Geranium Zonale—This is a decorative plant, very attractive when grown in pots and transplanted in the summer in a half-shady place in the garden, where they will bloom profusely. They are of all colors and are easily grown from seed, when sown in boxes.

Heliotrope—Mixed. This flower is loved by almost every one and is as easily grown from seed as the phlox or petunia. It is a strong grower and produces flowers in purple, lavender and white colors in profusion.

Mixed Verbena.

Give our Seeds a Trial and be convinced that what we say are facts.

Helichrysum Monstrosum Album and Rubrum—Red and white everlasting flower. Very showy double flowers, two feet high. December to April.

Helianthus Flora Pleno. — (Double Flowering Sunflower.) This variety grows about the same height as the large Russian Sunflower; but produces an abundance of flowers which are smaller in size, but very attractive. Said to be anti-malarious. Can be sown from February until June.

Russian Sunflower. — This is highly prized by poultry raisers and farmers as a cheap food for fowls. It is immensely productive and can be raised cheaper than corn, as any waste piece of ground will suffice. It is the best egg producing food known. The seed is also used here on a large scale for feeding hard-bill birds, such as the Red bird or Cardinal and Parrots, which are very fond of it.

Lobelia (*Erinus compacta*). — Very dwarf plants; growing four to six inches high and forming dense masses of blue flowers. Of easy culture and well adapted for bedding, edging, pots or rockeries. Sow October till April.

Mathiola (*Annua*).—Sweet scented stocks. A charming hardy annual, produces flowers from white to dark blue and crimson colors. Sow in rich soil from October till April.

Mesembryanthemum. Crystallinum. (Ice plant,)—This beautiful plant is splendid for growing in hanging baskets or for bedding. It has singular icy foliage. Sow February till April.

Mirabilis Jalapa (Marvel of Peru).—This is the well-known Four O'Clock of variegated and mixed colors. It grows as easily as weeds and is splendid to plant in garden spots, near fences and places where other flowering plants will not do well. They produce an abundance of flowers of brilliant colors. February till June.

Marigold, French Dwarf—A very dwarf growing compact plant which produces flowers of yellow and brown color. January till April.

Mignonette (*Reseda odorata*). — A quick growing annual, highly esteemed for its delicate fragrance. It grows most rapidly and produces the largest and finest spikes of blossoms during cool moist weather of early spring and fall months; but will bloom all summer if seed is sown in the Spring. Sow December till April.

Mimulus Tigrinus (Monkey flower).—Tender-looking plants, with peculiar shaped and brilliantly colored flowers, blotched and spotted in every conceivable manner. Do very well, if planted in half-shady place in the garden. Sow December till March.

Myosotis Palustris (*Forget-me-not*).—This charming little plant succeeds best in a half-shady position in the garden and requires sandy and moist soil. They produce small blue flowers in clusters.

Nemophila Insignis—Blue Grove Love. Of neat compact habit, free blooming, producing bright blue flowers with white center; of easy culture. Sow December till April.

Nigella Damascena — Love-in-a-mist. Very showy in foliage and flowers. The pretty blue and white flowers are surrounded by a delicate wreath of mossy foliage.

Nasturtiums (*Dwarf and Tall*).—Mixed colors. This plant is of easy culture, produces fine foliage and flowers of beautiful variegated colors; it can be trained on trellises, although it does not grow very high. The dwarf variety can be grown in pots or hanging baskets and are very ornamental.

Marigold, Tall African—This variety is strong in habit and produces larger flowers, yellow in color.

Papaver Somniferum—Double Poppy. This is the true Opium Poppy of extra large size, of different colors; very showy. October till April. Should not be transplanted.

Ranunculus, Flowered—Small double French variety. Double-fringed flowers. October till April.

Pansies (*Viola tricolor maxima*).—Large mixed Pansy. Pansy seed is a specialty with us. We have only the finest strains, in color and size, and the best of seed to be obtained.

Improved Giant Trimardeau—Remarkable for the large size of the flowers, which, however, are not so circular in form as the German varieties. Most of the flowers are marked with three large blotches or spots.

Large Mixed German Pansies—These are famous for their almost endless variety of charming shades of colors, united with good size and most perfect form of flowers. They bloom profusely and embrace all the solid or self-colors; delicately shaded flowers; five spotted and three spotted. Sow October till March.

Petunia Hybrida — Petunia. Splendid mixed hybrid varieties. A very decorative plant of various colors, well known to almost every lover of flowers. Plants are of spreading habit; about one foot high. January till May.

Phlox Drummondii — Drummond's Phlox. One of the best and most popular annuals in cultivation. Their various colors and length of flowering, with easy culture, make them favorites with every one. All fine colors mixed. One foot high. December till April.

Phlox Drummondii Grandiflora Alba—Pure white, some with purple or violet eye.

Phlox Drummondii Grandiflora Stellata Splendens—This is admitted to be the richest colored and most effective of all large flowered Phloxes. It combines all the good qualities of the Splendens, with the addition of a clearly defined, pure white star, which contrasts strikingly with the vivid crimson of the flowers.

Portulaca—A small plant of great beauty, and of the easiest culture. Does best in a well exposed situation, where it has plenty of sun. The flowers are of various colors, from white to bright scarlet and crimson. The plant is good for edging vases or pots; or where large plants are kept in tubs, the surface can be filled with this neat little genus of plants. Half foot high. February till August.

Portulaca Grandiflora, Fl. Pl.—Double Portulaca. The same variety of colors with semi-

Do not buy cheap and spurious seeds as it is only a loss of time and money.

Double White Zinnia.

Pyrethrum Aurea—Golden Feather. The flowers resemble Asters. It has bright yellow leaves. which makes it very showy if massed as a border.

Ricinus. (Castor Oil Bean)—Semi tropical plants, which are grown largely for their great size and picturesque foliage The plants are surmounted by large spikes of flowers and brilliantly colored spiny seed pods. March till May.

Sensitive Plant. (*Mimosa pudica*).—The Sensitive Plant is very chaste and elegant in foliage the leaves being delicately binated, while it bears small pink flowers in globose heads. It affords much amusement by its *sensitive* character —even when slightly touched the leaves instantly close and droop; easily grown.

Salvia Splendens—(*Large-flowering Scarlet Sage.*)—Under our hot summer sun, "this flame-colored beauty" *is the most gorgeous of all plants. For months the blaze of flaming scarlet is intensely brilliant, with great spikes of bloom completely concealing the foliage.* A single plant will carry as many as *two hundred spikes of flowers*, each spike ten to twelve inches in length.

Scabiosa (*Mourning Bride.*)—The old and well-known *Sweet Scabious* is not so generally cultivated as it deserves. The perfectly double flowers are useful for cutting; they are gracefully borne upon long slender stems, well above the foliage.

Sweet Sultan (*Centaurea suaveolens*).—The Yellow Sweet Sultan produces its handsome, brush-like, bright-yellow flowers in wonderful profusion. The flowers have long stems and keep well.

Torenia Fournieri—Charming plants for pot culture and in the open garden; are very attractive in beds or masses; exceedingly free bloomers. They produce lovely velvety-blue flowers, with three large spots of darkest blue and a bright yellow throat; bloom until frost. February till May.

Verbena Hybrida — Extra fine mixed. Free-flowering, hardy annuals, of low spreading rowth. Single plants in rich soil will cover a space three to four feet in diameter and furnish a sprofusion of flowers. The flower-heads are of good size and fine regular form, highly valued for cut-flower decoration. If the flowers are kept cut off before seeding. the plants will bloom much more freely. Of late years the plants raised from cuttings and sold by florists have become quite diseased. Plants grown from seed are not only cheaper, but are strong and vigorous in growth, with rich dark-green foliage, and continue in bloom until cut off by heavy frosts.

White Verbena—Flowers pure white and of fine fragrance

Italian Striped—Very showy; stripe flowers of many bright colors.

Vinca—Rosea and Alba. Splendid pot an bedding plants; eighteen inches high, with gloss green leaves and circular flowers.

Zinnias—No flowers are easier grown fro seed in the open ground and they are a beauty i the garden when planted in groups or masses They bloom during the whole summer. The have been improved upon so much that a majorit of the new varieties resemble the Dahlia from distance. Sow from February till August.

Choice Double Mixed—Double flowers of good form and quite large size; brilliant colors

Double White—Dahlia-like flowers. per fectly double and of the purest, snowy-white.

double and double flowers. Half foot high. February till August.

Primula Veris—Cowslip. An herbaceous plant of various colors, highly esteemed in Eurol e. Half a foot high. December till April.

Primula Chinensis—Chinese Primrose. A green-house plant which flowers profusely and continues to bloom for a long time; should be sown early to insure the plant flowering well. Different colors; mixed, per package, 25 cents. One and a half feet high. October till February.

If you want to make a success in gardening, buy Schindler's Seeds.

CLIMBERS.

Antigonum Leptopus (*Rosa Montana*).—This is one of the finest perennial climbers for the South. It is a native of Mexico and is well adapted to our climate. It is of rapid growth and produces long racemes of beautiful pink flowers. In the winter the vine should be cut down and the roots covered with moss or straw. Flowers freely the first year. Sow February till April.

Aristolochia Elegans. (Dutchman's Pipe).—This plant is of vigorous growth and is most suitable for the Southern States. It bears large flowers of a rich purple color, with irregular markings of creamy white and golden yellow center. This plant blooms when quite young and continues until killed by frost. Sow from January till March.

Benincasa Cerifera (Wax Gourd).—A strong growing vine with long-shaped dark crimson fruit, when ripe, has a fine musky odor; it is splendid for making preserves.

Balloon Vine (*Cardiospermum*).—The Balloon Vine or "Love-in-a-puff" is of rapid growth, with pretty foliage and inflated capsules or seed-pods,

Maurandia Barclayana.

Cobaea Scandens—Of rapid growth and large size, with fine foliage. Most graceful with large bell-shaped flowers of a beautiful violet hue.

Cypress Vine—Delicate fern-like foliage and beautiful star-shaped flowers.

Scarlet—Intensely rich scarlet.

White—Purest paper white.

Curcurbita—Ornamental Gourd. Mixed., This is a fine climber, making fine shade and producing gourds of all shapes and form. Sow February till April.

Curcurbita Lagenaria Dulcis—Sweet Gourd. This is a strong growing vine which produces long green club-like fruit, which makes a palatable dish when used green like squash.

Dolichos. (Hyacinth Bean).—Of extra rapid growth; runs from 20 to 30 feet high and produces purple and white flowers, which turn into purple beans. Very ornamental.

Evening Glory (*Ipomaea Bona Nox*).—This is of a rapid growth and produces large white flowers, which open in the evening; it is often advertised as the Moon-flower.

Maurandia Barclayana—Mixed Rapid growing vine producing rose, purple and white colored flowers and elegant foliage.

Mina Lobata—The flowers appear on fork-like racemes, rising almost erect out of the dense and luxuriant foliage; they are, as buds, at first bright red, but change through orange-yellow to yellowish-white when in full bloom. It is a quite rapid-growing climber, if started early in pots under glass.

Momordica Balsamina—Balsam Apple This is a beautiful delicate climber of luxuriant foliage; it produces a warty, elongated fruit, which when ripe turns red. The fruit, when ripe, is put into a glass jar with whiskey and is splendid for healing cuts and bruises. Sow March till May.

Mina Lobata.

Japanese Morning Glories.

Morning Glories. (*Imperial Japanese.*)— This is one of the greatest improvements of the common Morning Glory. They are of an increased size, of beautiful, variegated colors and some are fringed. The foliage is also very pretty, as some of the leaves are marbled with white and golden yellow spots. No garden should be without this marvelous flower. Sow February till May.

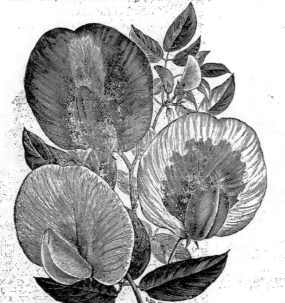

Momordica Balsamina.

Sweet Peas. (Mixed.)

Schindler & Co's Seeds are the Gardeners Choice.

White Sweet Peas.

Luffa Acutangula (*Dish Rag Vine*).—A rapid growing vine, with large foliage; splendid for making shade or covering unsightly out-houses or walls. It produces long green fruit which when dry, can be used for washing dishes; also in making ornamental baskets.

Sweet Peas (Mixed).—This flowering pea is too well known to be described. Our mixture consists of all the finest and lately introduced varieties and cannot be surpassed for quality.

Blanche Burpee (Pure White).—A grand, large flower of pure whiteness Vines are of strong growth, blooming profusely throughout the season.

FLOWERING BULBS.

Anemones.—Double Flowering. The roots should be planted in spring and fall, in pots, boxes or the open ground. Of different colors, fine for planting in masses with hyacinths and Ranunculus. Price, 30c. per doz.

Calla Lily. (*Lily of the Nile.*)—This is a beautiful pot plant and is very ornamental when in bloom for home culture. The proper time to plant them is in October and November; they can also be planted throughout winter and spring. They require a great deal of moisture; they are splendid for fish ponds and fountains and thrive well if the pot is half elevated above the water.

Price 25c.

Chinese Sacred Lilies.—This is one of the finest bulbs for in-door culture. It should be planted in a bowl or wide dish, in which gravel stones or pieces of brick have been put in place; then fill the bowl a little over half full of water and place in a dark room for two or three weeks to draw root, after which it can be gradually brought

to the light, and will bloom shortly thereafter. It produces beautiful flowers on trusses, pure white in color, with yellow center.

Price, 15c each.

Calla Lily.

Dahlias.—This is one of the leading bulbs grown in the South especially in the vicinity of New Orleans; they are grown mostly for flowers for "All Saints" day. The roots we offer are all of double flowers and of all colors. Should not be planted before latter part of March, beginning of April.

Price 25c each, $2.50 per doz.

Gladiolus.—These summer-flowering bulbs are easily grown and produce a great display of brilliant flowers at small expense. Our stock is grown from the most beautiful French hybrid varieties, embracing a grand range of the most beautiful shades of colors. combined with large size and fine open form of flowers.

Price 50c per doz.

Gloxinias (*Hybrida.*)—This is one of the finest and easiest grown bulbs for window-pot culture for the South They do very well in half shady situations and produce beautiful bell-shaped flowers of all colors. a good percentage being variegated. The leaves are an ornament for their velvety texture. When in bloom they require a good deal of moisture. Plant early in spring in sandy soil.

Price 25c each.

Hyacinths.—This is one of the easiest out-door bulbs to plant. They are double and single flowering of red, blue, white, pink and yellow colors Plant from October till March. They can also be easily grown in pots or in bottles with

Double Dahlias.

water. If put in bottles, use a pickle jar with the mouth large enough to rest the bulb on top; fill with water and put in a dark room for two or

three weeks; then put it gradually to the light and in a short time it will bloom.

Price 50c and 75c per doz.

Narcissus. — Double White, Paper-White, Trumpet-Major. These are fine bulbs for open-ground planting for early winter and spring flowers. They require no attention after being planted. Should be planted from October till February.

Price 40c. per doz.

HARDY JAPANESE LILIES.

Lilium Auratum.

Lilium Auratum (*The Golden-Banded Lily of Japan*).—*This is the largest and finest of all Lilies.* The grand open star-like flowers frequently measure ten inches in diameter and are delightfully fragrant The petals are a clear ivory-white, banded with rich golden yellow and heavily spotted at base with deep crimson.

Price 20c. each.

Lilium Longiflorum.—A hardy variety having long, trumpet-like, pure white flowers. identical with those of the well-known *Bermuda* or *Easter-Lily* It is of strong growth and later in flowering when planted in the open ground.

Price 15c each.

Lilium speciosum Monstrosum Album. The flower-stalks of this variety are broad and flattened. The flowers of large size are purest white, with petals heavily reflexed.

Price 20c each.

Lilium Speciosum Rubrum or Roseum. — Very hardy and free flowering Flowers of large size and fine open star-like form, with petals well reflexed; the petals are white shaded with deep rose.

Price 15c. each.

Gladiolus Mixed.

Merchants write to us for special prices on seeds in large quantities.

Tuberoses.

Lilium Tigrinum Flore Pleno (*Double Tiger* ‎‎‎‎‎‎ ‎‎‎‎‎‎ variety is of strong growth and great ▓▓▓▓▓▓ looming, while each flower is quite double, having several rows of showy tigered petals.

Price 15c each.

Scilla Peruviana.—These bulbs produce fine blue and white flowers, which are borne on a long stem and formed like a truss. They are of easy culture; should be planted in large pots and taken into the house when the thermometer predicts freezing. It is one of the most beautiful flowering bulbs known and is worthy of a trial. Plant October till February.

Price 25c. each.

Tulips. (*Double and Single*).—This bulb is easily grown and only flowers to perfection, when we have a severe winter or snow weather. Stil the bulbs are so cheap that anyone can risk to grow them during winter for their handsome flowers. Do not cover too deep and plant from November to February.

Price 40c doz.

Tuberoses.—Large Double. This produces a fine cluster of pure white flowers, which grow upright on a single stem. Very useful for making bouquets and floral work of all kinds. It is very fragrant and is easily grown in the open ground.

Price 40c doz.

MISCELLANEOUS

Vegetable Pear (*Sechium Edule*).—This vegetable is generally called "*Mirliton*" in our market. It makes a rapid growing vine, with grape-like leaves. The fruit is used like squash or egg-plant. It has only one seed which is enclosed in the bulb and the whole fruit has to be planted. Price 10c. each. Should be planted in March and April.

Rhubarb Roots—Splendid for making pies; should be planted early in spring or in fall. When once established will remain and thrive for several years.

FIG TREES.

Celestial, OR Celeste Fig—This is the only variety and best for our latitude: it is enormously productive, easily grown and its fruit is always in demand in our markets. We consider it one of the most profitable fruits which can be grown South. It is used to quite an extent for canning purposes. Price, 1 year old 25c. each, $2.50 doz.

STRAWBERRIES.

This is one of the easiest and finest fruits to grow for family use as well for the market; no family garden should be without them. They thrive best in a rich sandy loam. Where this cannot be had, a good mixture of horse-manure, well plowed under and the soil well pulverized, will have the desired effect in growing fine, large berries. They should be set out from October till February. The best varieties for our section of country are the Hoffmann seedling, Cloud and Michel's Early. Price 50c. per 100; $4.50 per 1000. Price for larger quantities given upon application.

ARTICHOKE PLANTS.

We can furnish strong healthy plants in large quantities during proper seasons, these plants, if set out in October, November, December, will produce a fair crop of fruit in spring. Can be set out until end of February.

Price 25c. per doz.; $1.50 per 100.

Give our Seeds a Trial and be convinced that what we say are facts.

BIRD SEEDS.

We make a specialty in putting up extra cleaned Canary seed (mixed or plain) in cartoons containing one pound, including a piece of cuttle-fish bone. Our mixture contains CANARY, HEMP, RAPE and GERMAN MILLET SEEDS. We also have in bulk Hemp, Canary, Rape, Millet and Sunflower seeds.

RAFFIA.

This is the best material for tying plants of all kinds to stakes, as it is not apt to rot as quickly as twine; it is splendid for tying bunches of vegetables of all kinds for market. Price 30c. per lb.

GRAFTING WAX.

Lion Brand—This is the best wax to use for grafting and budding trees and roses. ¼ lb. 15c., 1 lb. 40c.

The Perfection Jr!, Broadcast Seed Sower—The cheapest and best seed sower on the market. Price $1.25 each. No gardener or farmer will sow seed by hand any more, if he can buy a seed-sower at such a low price. They save seed, time, labor and distribute the seed more uniformly than by hand.

ALBERT'S PLANT FOOD.

BEST FERTILIZER FOR HOUSE PLANTS.

This is a scientific preparation containing in a highly concentrated and easily soluble form, the food element required by plants. It is odorless, clean to handle, quick in its action and unequaled in its effects. Inside each tin is a SMALL SPOON holding the exact quantity for dissolving in a quart of water. By its use plants acquire a sturdier growth, fuller developments and a manifold increase in bloom. For palms, ferns, India-rubber plants, it is by far the most complete, most effective, most economical and easiest applied fertilizer made. The analysis is as high as it is possible to make a chemical Plant Food, which at the same time can be used without risk of injury to the plants. It is put up in neat tins as shown in cut, and full directions are given on outside of each box. Can be safely mailed.

Price, 15c. each. Postage 8c. extra.

TOBACCO DUST.

This is one of the best and cheapest insect destroyers known. It is also a good fertilizer. If you are troubled with *cabbage* flies and lice, also fleas and lice on cucumbers, melons and tomatoes. use Tobacco Dust and you will get rid of them in a few applications. It also acts as a fertilizer, as it contains a good percentage of potash and ammonia. Price per package, 10 pounds, 25c; 50 pounds, $1.00; per 100 pound sack, $1.50.

WHALE OIL SOAP.

Very effective for cleansing trees of all kinds of insects and fungi; it is also a fine remedy for destroying insects and lice on plants of all sorts. Use one pound soap in two quarts hot water, then dilute same; after this add 5 or 6 gallons cold water and sprinkle or spray trees or plants. Splendid for killing the Aphides on fruit trees.

FRENCH SCYTHE BLADES.

We have a fine assortment of these valuable blades, which are of direct importation and considered the best scythe by professional mowers. We have different sizes and qualities; they range from 18 to 24 inches; the blue are a little higher in price.

Prices, Blue.—18-in., 85c; 22-in., 90c; 24-in., $1.00.

Prices, Plain —18-in., 75c.; 20-in., 80c.; 22-in., 85c; 24-in., 90c.

We also have these blades *bridled or strengthened* which cost 35c. each extra.

The best and cheapest Hand Spray Pump.

The Electric Bug Exterminator Brass. Price $1.25 each.

This is one of the best and cheapest exterminators ever invented. It is durable, simple and easily handled. They are superior to any other bug or insect exterminator on the market. You can use Kerosene, Paris green, London purple or any other solution with the sprayer without any danger of injuring the plants.

FINGER SPADES.

This tool is made to save the finger nails in weeding out all obnoxious weeds and grasses which generally grow between vegetable and flower plants. No one should be without them, as they are so cheap. Only 10c. each.

Schindler & Co's Seeds are the Gardeners Choice.

HAMMOND'S SLUG SHOT.

SLUG SHOT KILLS BUGS.—(EITHER DUSTED OR SPRAYED.)
SLUG SHOT KILLS THE POTATO BUG AND SOW BUG—(OR ROLLER)

It is a fine insecticide; if used in a dry state for destroying fleas, lice and caterpillars of all kinds on Cabbage plants, Turnips, Lettuce and all other vegetable plants attacked by insects. It also destroys potato bugs and grub worms. On all garden plants dust the Slug Shot lightly and thoroughly; for vine crops, put more on the ground, around the stems, than on the leaves for Melons, Squash and Cucumbers. Apply in the morning when the dew is on the plants or dust after a rain; in case of dry weather, give the plants a good watering in the evening and then dust the slug shot.

Price, 5 lbs. pkge. 30c. Prices for larger quantities given upon application. We also have DUSTERS for distributing Slug Shot Powder with very fine perforated bottoms, insures economical distribution. Half Gallon size, price 35 cents. One Gallon size, price 50 cents.

Ladies Favorite Pruning Shears.

Scollay's Hand Rubber Sprinkler.

SCOLLAY'S RUBBER HAND SPRINKLER.

A fine and handy device for sprinkling floral work, cut flowers or pot plants. Very useful for dampening clothes or any kind of sprinkling. Made of the best rubber and with little care will last for years. Never gets out of order. They are so cheap, that no one should be without it. Price by Mail, post-paid, Largest size, $1.1 ; Medium size 70c.; small size, 60c.

LADIES' FAVORITE PRUNING SHEARS.

One of the handiest tools for pruning Rose bushes, shrubbery and plants of all kinds; also for cutting flowers. It is made of the best steel, highly polished and so small and light, that it can be carried conveniently in the pocket.

Price........................$1.00 each.

Slug Shot is the most effective Bug and Worm Destroyer.

FLORAL DESIGNS.

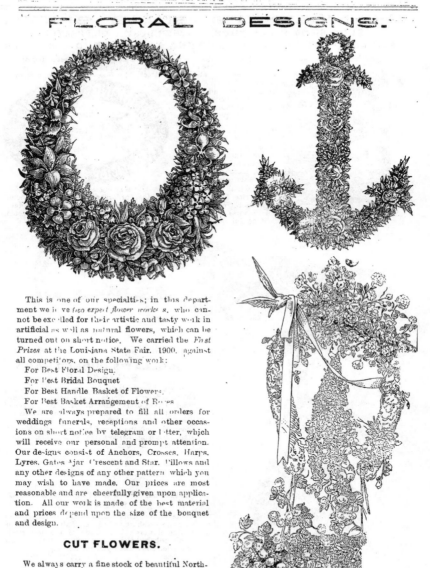

This is one of our specialties; in this depart-ment we have two expert flower workers, who can-not be excelled for their artistic and tasty work in artificial as well as natural flowers, which can be turned out on short notice. We carried the First Prizes at the Louisiana State Fair, 1900, against all competitors, on the following work:

For Best Floral Design.
For Best Bridal Bouquet.
For Best Handle Basket of Flowers.
For Best Basket Arrangement of Roses.

We are always prepared to fill all orders for weddings, funerals, receptions and other occas-ions on short notice by telegram or letter, which will receive our personal and prompt attention. Our designs consist of Anchors, Crosses, Harps, Lyres, Gates Ajar, Crescent and Star, Pillows and any other designs of any other pattern which you may wish to have made. Our prices are most reasonable and are cheerfully given upon applica-tion. All our work is made of the best material and prices depend upon the size of the bouquet and design.

CUT FLOWERS.

We always carry a fine stock of beautiful North-ern flowers, such as Brides and Bridesmaid Roses, White and Pink Carnations, Lilies of the Valley, Adiantums or Maiden Hair Ferns, Asparagus Plumosis and Fancy Fern Leaves, which we can always furnish on short notice at reasonable Price.

FLORAL WIRE FRAMES

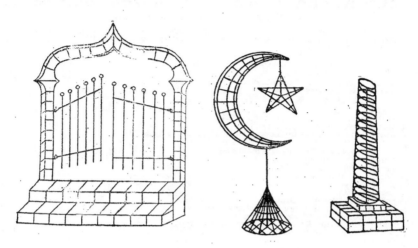

We are headquarters for wire frames of all kinds for floral designs and are in a position to turn out any design or pattern submitted to us, on the shortest notice. Our prices are reasonable and workmanship first-class. We carry in stock the following designs: Wreaths, Anchors, Crosses, Lyres, Gates Ajar, Harps, Crescent and Star, Crescent and Lyre, with or without stands; Broken Columns, Pillows, Scrolls and from 8 to 36 inches

All our Wire Frames and Designs are made by first-class and expert wire-workers and all our work is made on short notice and with promptness.

Prices given upon application.

RETAIL PRICE LIST
SCHINDLER & CO'S RELIABLE GARDEN SEEDS
——WE MAIL SEEDS POSTAGE PAID.——

Seeds in Packets, Ounces and Quarter Pounds mailed by us free of postage. On Half Pounds, Pounds, Pints and Quarts the postage must be added to the prices quoted at the rate of 8 cents per pound and 16 cents per quart.

VARIETIES.		PRICES.	

ARTICHOKE.

	Per Ounce.	Per ¼ lb.	Per lb.
Large Green Globe (Loan)	$0 35	$1 00	$3 50

Artichoke plants per doz 25c; per 100, $1.50; per 1000, $12.00, by express.

ASPARAGUS.

Conover's Colossal	10	15	50
Palmetto	10	20	
Mammoth Columbia	10	20	75

Roots, 2 yrs old either kind, express, per 100, 75c; per 1,000, $5.00.
" " " " " "   25c. per dozen.

BEANS. Dwarf, Snap or Bush.

	Per qt.	Per peck.	Per bushel
Extra Early Refugee	25	1 50	5 00
Early Mohawk Six Weeks	20	1 25	4 50
Early Yellow Six Weeks	20	1 25	4 50
Red Kidney	20	1 25	4 00
Best of All	25	1 25	4 50
Extra Early Red Valentine	25	1 25	4 50
Improved Dwarf German Wax (stringless)	25	1 75	6 00
Grenell's Improved Dwarf Golden Wax	25	1 75	6 00
Wardwell's Dwarf Kidney Wax(crop very short)	75	4 00	12 00
Dwarf Flageolet or Perfection Wax	30	1 75	6 50
Davis Kidney Wax	35	2 25	8 00
Henderson's Bush Lima	30	2 25	7 50
Burpee's Bush Lima	30	2 25	8 00
New Stringless Green-pod	25	1 50	5 50
French Market Round Green-pod (crop very short)	75c. quart, $2.50 per gallon.		

BEANS—Pole or Running.

Large Lima	30	1 75	6 75
Carolina or Sieva	30	1 75	6 7
Siebert's Early Lima	50	2 50	10 00
Dutch Case Knife	35	2 00	6 50
Southern Prolific	25	1 50	6 00
Crease Back	30	2 00	7 00
Lazy Wife's	40	2 00	7 00

BEANS—English.

Broad Windsor	20	1 00	3 50

BEETS.

Schindler's Extra Early Red Turnip	10	25	75
Dewing's Early Red Turnip	10	20	40
Detroit Early Blood Turnip	10	20	50
Half Long Blood	10	20	40
Edmands Early Blood Turnip	10	20	50
Crosby's Egyptian	10	20	60
Egyptian Red Turnip, Extra Early	10	20	50
Eclipse	10	20	40
Lentz	10	20	[50
Long Red Mangel Wurzel	10	20	40
White French or Sugar	10	20	40
Silver, or Swiss Chard	10	20	60

BORECOLE or Curled Kale.

	Per oz.	Per ¼ lb.	Per lb.
Dwarf German Greens	15	35	1 00
Broccoli Purple Cape	25	1 00	3 25
Brussels Sprouts	20	50	1 75

CABBAGE.

Early York	$0 15	$0 40	$1 50
Large York	15	40	1 50
Large Oxheart	20	50	1 50
Early Winningstadt	20	50	1 75
Jersey Wakefield	20	65	2 00

Charleston Wakefield	25	60	2 00
All Seasons	20	65	2 00
Danish Ball Head	25	75	2 50
Stein's Early Large Flat Dutch, very fine	25	65	2 00
Solid South	25	75	3 00
Succession, Henderson's True Genuine	25	1 00	3 00
Large Flat Brunswick, German Imported	25	65	2 00
Improved Large Late Drumhead	25	65	2 00
Schindler's Superior Large Late Flat Dutch	25	65	2 50
Frotscher's Superior Large Late Flat Dutch	25	65	2 00
Crescent City Large Late Flat Dutch	25	65	2 00
Improved Early Summer, Henderson's	25	65	2 50
Red Dutch (for pickling) Mammoth Rock	20	50	2 00
Green Globe Savoy	20	50	2 00
Early Dwarf Savoy	20	50	2 00
Drumhead Savoy	20	65	2 00
Early All Head	25	75	2 00

CAULIFLOWER.

Extra Early Paris	75	2 00	7 50
Half Early Paris	75	2 00	7 50
Early Erfurt	1 00	2 25	10 00
Early Snowball, True	2 00	6 50	22 00
Le Normand Short Stemmed	75	2 25	9 00
Early Italian Giant	75	2 00	7 50
Late Italian Giant	75	2 00	7 50
Large Algiers, fine French Strain (Pure)	1 00	3 00	10 00

CARROTS.

Early Scarlet Horn	10	25	75
Half Long Scarlet French	10	25	90
Half Long Luc	10	25	90
Improved Long Orange	10	25	75
Long Red, without core	10	25	90
St. Valerie	10	25	90
Danver's Intermediate	10	25	75
Chantenay, Half Long	10	25	90

CELERY.

	Per oz.	Per ¼ lb.	Per lb.
White Plume	25	60	1 75
Large White Solid (finest American)	20	60	1 75
Perfection Heartwell (very fine)	20	50	1 50
Dwarf Large Ribbed	20	60	1 75
Golden Self-Blanching (French grown)	40	1 25	4 00
Giant Pascal	20	50	1 75
Celeriac, or Turnip-Rooted	20	40	1 50
Cutting or Soup	10	30	1 00
Flavoring Celery (not for sowing)	5	15	30

CHERVIL.

Plain-Leaved	15	40	1 50

COLLARDS. Georgia

COLLARDS. Georgia	15	40	1 00

CORN SALAD

CORN SALAD	15	40	1 00

CORN.

	Per qt.	Per peck	Per bushel
Extra Early Dwarf Sugar	$0 30	$1 75	$6 00
Adam's Extra Early	20	1 00	3 50
Southern Express	20	90	3 00
French Market—Best Early	25	1 00	3 50
Large Adams Early	25	1 00	3 00
White St. Charles	20	60	2 00
Mexican June	25	1 00	3 00
Yellow Creole in ears 5c. each—$2.50 per 100			
Early Sugar or Sweet	30	1 75	6 00
Stowell's Evergreen Sugar	30	1 75	6 00
Golden Beauty	15	60	2 00
Champion White Pearl	15	60	2 00
Golden Dent Gourd Seed	15	60	2 00
Early Yellow Canada	15	65	2 00
Large White Flint	15	65	2 00
Blount's Prolific Field	15	65	2 25
Improved Leaming	15	65	2 00
Mosby's Prolific	20	75	2 50
Hickory King (White)	25	1 75	6 00
White Rockdale	25	75	2 50
Black Mexican	25	1 50	5 50

(CORN column note in margin: By mail, add 15c. per quart for postage.)

N. B.—Prices for larger quantities given on application.

Our Cucumber Seeds are money-makers and True to Name.

CUCUMBER.

Improved Early White Spine	20	60	2 25
New Orleans Market	35	1 00	3 00
Early Frame	20	60	2 25
Long Green Turkey	20	65	2 00
Early Cluster	25	65	2 00
Japanese Climbing (very prolific)	35	1 00	3 50
Gherkin, or Burr (for pickling)	25	75	2 25
Prolific Pickling	25	75	2 50

EGGPLANT.

Large Purple, or New Orleans Market	50	1 50	5 00
Early Dwarf Oval	30	1 25	4 00
New York Market (Thornless)	40	1 25	4 00

ENDIVE.

Green Curled	20	60	2 00
Extra Fine Curled	20	60	2 00
Broad-leaved, or Escarolle	20	60	2 00

GARLIC Sets. 35c. qt.

KOHLRABI.

Early White Vienna, finest	25	1 00	3 00

LEEK.

Large London Flag (American grown)	15	50	1 50
Large Carentan	20	60	2 00
Large Rouen	20	60	1 75

LETTUCE.

California Cream Butter	20	50	2 00
Improved Royal Cabbage	20	50	1 25
Brown Dutch	20	40	1 50
Drumhead Cabbage	15	40	1 25
White Paris Coss	20	50	2 00
N. O. Improved Large Passion	20	60	2 00
Schindler's Early Market, none better	20	60	2 00
Trocadero French Imported	20	60	2 00
Big Boston	20	60	2 00

Melon, Musk or CANTELOUPE.

Rockyford (Colorado grown seed)	15	40	1 00
Netted Citron	10	35	90
Pine Apple	15	40	90
New Orleans Market	20	50	1 00
Osage	15	40	90
Early Hackensack	15	30	1 00
Paul Rose or Petoskey	15	40	1 00
Cannon Ball or Metropolitan	15	40	90
Emerald Gem	15	50	1 50

MELON, WATER.

	Ice Cream, (White Seeded)	10	20	60
	Dark Icing	10	20	60
Southern grown Sup. Quality.	Rattlesnake (true)	10	25	75
	Pride of Georgia	10	25	75
	Mammoth Iron-Clad	10	25	75
	Kolb Gem	10	25	75
	Florida's Favorite	10	25	75
	Seminole	10	25	75
	Lone Star (Genuine)	15	30	90

MUSTARD.

Southern Curled	10	20	60
Chinese Large Leaved	10	20	
White or Yellow Seeded	5	15	

NASTURTIUM.

Tall	15	30	1 00
Dwarf	15	30	00

OKRA.

Green Tall Growing	10	20	60

We can confidently recommend our Melon Seed to be first-class.

Extra Early Dwarf Green Prolific	10	20	60
White Velvet	10	20	60
French Market	10	25	75

ONION.

	Per Ounce.	Per ¼ lb.	
Frotscher's Creole	20	60	2 00
New Queen	25	75	2 50

ITALIAN ONION.

Bermuda (true) Red and White (Teneriffe grown)	25	75	3 00
The Prize Taker	20	60	2 00

ONION SETS.

	Per quart	Per gallon.	Per peck.	Per bush.
White, Western	20	60	1 25	2 50
Red or Yellow	15	50	75	2 00
Creole	20	60	1 00	3 00
SHALLOTS. White	20	50	1 00	2 50

PARSLEY.

	Per Ounce.	Per ¼ lb.	Per lb.
Creole	15	40	1 00
Plain Leaved	10	20	60
Double Curled	10	20	60
Improved Garnishing	10	25	70
Market Gardeners Curled	10	25	70
PARSNIP.—Hollow Crown or Sugar	10	20	60

PEAS.

	Per pt.	Per qt.	Per gallon.	Per peck.	Per bush.
Extra Early (First an 'est)	15	25	75	1 50	6 00
Early Alaska	15	25	80	1 50	6 00
Tom Thumb	15	30	90	1 75	6 00
Early Washington	15	25	75	1 50	6 00
Blue Beauty	25	40	1 00	1 75	6 50
Laxton's Alpha	25	40	1 00	1 50	6 00
Champion of England	20	30	90	1 50	5 00
Carter's Stratagem	25	40	1 00	2 00	7 50
Carter's Telephone	25	40	1 00	2 00	6 55
McLean's Little Gem	25	40	1 00	2 00	7 05
Dwarf Blue Imperial	15	25	75	1 50	5 55
Royal Dwarf Marrow	15	20	50	1 25	3 70
Black-Eyed Marrowfat	15	20	50	1 25	3 70
Large White Marrowfat	15	20	50	1 25	3 70
American Wonder	20	40	1 25	2 50	7 50

By mail, add 8c. per pint & 15c. per quart for postage.

Field or Cow Peas.   Market Price.

PEPPER.

	Per Ounce	Per ¼ lb.	Per lb.
Bell or Bull Nose	25	60	2 00
Sweet Spanish Monstrous (True)	25	1 00	3 00
Long Red Cayenne	25	75	2 50
Red Cherry	25	75	2 25
Golden Dawn Mango	25	75	3 00
Bird Eye	50	1 50	5 00
Chili	30	75	2 50
Genuine Tabasco	50	1 50	5 00
Ruby King, Sweet	25	75	2 50
Red Cluster	50	1 50	5 00

POTATOES.

	Per peck	Per bush.	Per barrel
Boston Peerless	50	1 50	4 00
White Elephant	75	2 00	4 50
Extra Early Vermont	75	2 00	4 50
Vermont Early Rose	75	2 00	4 00
Snowflake	75	2 00	4 00
Improved Beauty of Hebron	75	2 00	4 00
Eastern Burbanks	75	1 50	3 75
White Star	50	1 75	4 00
Early Ohio	75	2 00	4 00

Prices subject to fluctuation

These are all Eastern grown, true to name, and of the finest
stocks ever offered in this market.

Early Triumph, Tennessee grown, Genuine	75	2 00	4 50

(Drayage extra.)

POTATOES, SWEET.

Yellow Pumpkin, Yam	60	2 00	3 50
Spanish Yam	50	1 75	3 50
Southern Queen	40	1 50	3 50
Shanghai or California Yam	40	1 25	3 00

Prices vary according to market.

Schindler's Seeds are most reliable.

PUMPKIN.	Per Ounce	Per ¼ lb.	Per lb.
Kentucky field	$ 10	20	$0 60
Large Cheese	10	20	60
Frotscher's Cashaw Crook-Neck (green striped) true	15	35	90
Golden Yellow Mammoth or Tours	15	30	1 00
Connecticut Field	10	20	50
RADISH,			
Long White Lady-finger	10	20	60
Early Long Scarlet	10	20	50
Early Scarlet Turnip, White Tipped	10	20	60
Yellow Summer Turnip, or Golden Globe	10	20	60
Early Scarlet Olive Shaped	10	20	50
White Summer Turnip	10	20	60
Scarlet Half Long French	10	20	50
Scarlet, Olive Shaped. White Tipped or French Breakfast	10	20	60
Black Spanish, Winter	10	20	60
Chinese Rose, Winter	10	20	60
Chartier	10	20	60
White Strassburg	10	20	60
Long Brightest Scarlet (French Grown)	10	20	60
ROQUETTE	25	75	2 50
SALSIFY.			
Sandwich Island Mammoth	15	40	1 50
SORREL. Broad-leaved	15	50	1 50
SPINACH.			
Extra-Large-leaved Savoy	10	20	35
Broad-leaved Flanders	10	20	30
SQUASH.			
Early Bush, or Patty Pan	10	30	80
Long Green, or Summer Crook-Neck	10	25	75
London Vegetable Marrow	15	50	1 50
The Hubbard	15	50	1 25
Boston Marrow	15	30	90
TOMATO.			
Ponderosa	35	1 00	3 50
Trophy, selected	25	60	2 25
Acme	25	60	2 25
Paragon	25	50	2 00
Livingston's Stone	25	65	2 25
" Perfection	25	65	2 00
" Favorite	25	65	2 25
" Beauty	25	65	2 25
Dwarf Champion	25	75	2 50
Atlantic Prize. Extra Early	25	75	2 50
TURNIP.	Per oz.	Per ¼ lb.	Per lb.
Early Red or Purple Top, (strap-leaved)	10	20	50
Early White Flat Dutch, (strap-leaved)	10	20	50
Large White Globe	10	20	50
Yellow Aberdeen	10	20	50
Golden Ball	10	20	60
Amber Globe	10	20	50
Improved Purple Top Ruta Baga, Long Island Grown	10	20	50
Munich Early Purple Top	10	25	70
Purple Top Globe	10	20	50
Extra Early White Egg	10	25	70
White Hanover	10	20	50
Cow Horn	10	20	60

SWEET and MEDICINAL HERBS.

Anise, Balm, Basil, Bene, Borage, Caraway, Coriander, Dill, Fennel, Horehound, Lavender, Marjoram, Pot Marigold, Tansy, Rosemary, Rue, Sage, Summer Savory, Thyme, Wormwood........} Per pack, 5 cents

GRASS and FIELD SEEDS.	Per lb	Per ½ bu.	Per bush.
Red Clover	15	5 00	9 00
White Dutch Clover	25	7.50	14 00
Alfalfa or French Lucerne	25	7 00	12 00
Crimson Clover	15	3 00	5 00
Lespedeza Striata or Japan Clover	20	2 25	4 00
Kentucky Blue Grass, Fancy	15	1 00	2 00

Schindler's Seeds are the most reliable.

Red Top Grass, Choice......	15	90	1 50
English Rye Grass	10	1 00	2 00
Mixed Lawn Grass	20	1 75	3 00
Johnson Grass, Extra Cleaned......	15	1 75	2 50
Orchard Grass. Choice......	20	1 50	2 50
Timothy	15	2 00	3 50
Kaffir Corn......	10	1 00	1 50
Texas Rye	10	75	1 20
Texas Barley......	10	75	1 20
Texas Red Rust Proof Oats	10	45	75
Broom Corn......	10	1 50	2 50
Buckwheat......	10	1 50	2 50
Russian Sunflower	15	1 00	1 75
Hairy Vetch......	20	4 00	7 50
Winter Turf Oats	10	65	1 25
Giant Beggar Weed......	30	10 lbs. for 2 50

Australian Salt Bush...........................Per packet, 10c. 15c oz. $1.25 lb.
Dwarf Essex Rape..................................1 lb 20c. ; 8 lbs $1.00.

Italian Rye Grass......	10.	1 50	2 50
German Millet......	10	1 00	1 50
Early Amber Sorghum	10	1 25	2 00
Orange Sorghum......	10	1 25	2 00

Velvet Beans ....Peck 75c., bushel $2.75
Bermuda Grass (Genuine) ... .¼ lb. 35c., per lb. $1.00
Spanish Peanuts ....15c. per lb., $2.00 per bushel
Sainfoin or Esparsette...........................15 per lb., 10 lbs. $1 00.
Teosinte...¼ lb. 35c. ; per lb. $1.25 postpaid
White Virginia Peanuts ....15c. lb., $2.00 per bushel
Red Tennessee Peanuts ....15c. lb., $2.00 per bushel
Jerusalem Artichoke ....65c. Peck, $2.25 per bushel
Rhubarb Roots ....20c. each, per dozen $1.50
Burr or California Clover (Measured).............quart 10c. ; bushel $2.00

Vegetable Plants.

CHIVES (Schnittlauch) ....20c. bunch
Cabbage (Best Varieties)..........................60c per 100, $4 50 per 1000
Cauliflower (Best Varieties)......................$1.00 per 100 ; $7.50 per 1000
Eggplants, " " ....$1.50 per 100 ; $10.00 per 1000
Tomatoes, " " ....$1.00 per 100 ; $7.50 per 1000
Sweet Pepper, Best Varieties... ....$1.50 per 100 ; $10.00 per 1000
Hot Pepper, " " ....$1.50 per 100 ; $10.00 per 1000

We make no charge for cartage, bags, boxes or packing, excepting on Potatoes and Grass Seeds, **but at these prices buyer must pay all Express or Freight charges.** Small parcels can go by mail if purchaser desires it. In such cases 8 cents for each pound and 15 cents for each quart must be added to these prices to cover postage.

These prices are subject to change as season advances, depending on shortage or surplus of stock.

READE'S ELECTRIC ANT DESTROYER.
(READE'S)
Rids Closets, Houses and Grounds of Ants and Worms of all sorts in Gardens and Flower Pots.
Price in bottles at 25c. and 50c. each.

THE GARDENERS' FRIEND.
READE'S ELECTRIC WORM ERADICATOR.
TRADE MARK. **PERFECTLY ODORLESS.** REAJE)

For the Instantaneous Extermination of worms of every size and kind, Caterpillars, Flies, Ants, Scales, Red Spiders, Mealy Bugs, Green Fly, Snails, Lice and Wood Lice; Slugs and Grubs on Rose Bushes.
Sold in bottles at 50c., $1.00 and $3.00 each.

WEEDS UTTERLY DESTROYED.
"READE MFG. CO'S "HERBICIDE."
TRADE MARK. (READE)

Guttters, Paths and Roadways will keep clear of Weeds, Poison Ivy Grasses, Mosses, Dandelions, Burdocks, etc. for two full years or more. Its application is easy, being in a liquid form, and only requiring to be mixed with water and applied with a watering can or watering cart. Full directions for use with each package.

In quart cans, sufficient to make 5 gallons of liquid........................	$ .50
" ½ gal. " " " 10 " "	.80
" gallon " " " 20 " "	1.50
" 5 gal. kegs " " 100 " "	5.00
" 10 gal. " " " 200 " "	9.50

INDEX.

best

become exhausted

and before the new has started.   entirely

easier grown than the Spanish Peanut, it is very
cultivation when started.

con-

Cultivating. Peanuts should be planted at the same time in spring when Beans are
proper way is to plant the

Finocchio.

Rabarbaro.

Zafferano

Atanasia.

9 780260 498205